Dear Kilroy

Dear
Kilroy
A DOG TO GUIDE US

Nora Vitz Harrison

A Capital Discoveries Book

Capital Books, Inc.
Sterling, Virginia

"Mellow Yellow" Copyright © 1996, Donovan Music Limited. Copyright renewed. All rights reserved.
"Kilroy and Alice" and parts of "Eleanor" were previously published in *The Oregonian*, Portland, Oregon. "Saffron and the Woman on the Train" was previously published in *The News-Review*, Roseburg, Oregon.
All photos by Nora Vitz Harrison (© 2003 by Nora Vitz Harrison. All rights reserved) except as noted—Page 2: "Max," Thom Ainsworth*; Page 28: "Chain link Lab," Patricia N. Olson; Page 48: "Nash," Ed Smith*; Page 56: "Grace," Lin Hayes; Page 101: "Lab and cat," Richard Yoder; Page 124: "Pup entertaining self," Tracey Helmboldt; Page 171: "Guide dog puppies," Thom Ainsworth*; Page 181: "Riley and Nora," Tracey Helmboldt. Printed with permission.

* Courtesy of Guide Dogs for the Blind, Inc.

Photo electronic editing by Paul Zegers.

ISBN 1-931868-39-5 (alk. paper)
Library of Congress Cataloging-in-Publication Data
Harrison, Nora Vitz.
    Dear Kilroy : a dog to guide us / Nora Vitz Harrison – 1st ed.
      p. cm.
    ISBN 1-931868-39-5
    1. Dogs–Oregon–Anecdotes. 2. Dog owners–Oregon–Anecdotes. 3. Harrison, Nora Vitz.
    4. Human-animal relationships–Oregon–Anecdotes. I. Title.

SF426.2 H366 2003
636.7–dc21
2002041313
Printed in the United States of America on acid-free paper that meets the American National Standards Institute Z39-48 Standard.
First Edition
10 9 8 7 6 5 4 3 2 1

FOR ELEANOR

who loved all living things

By ethical conduct toward all creatures,
we enter into a spiritual relationship
with the universe.

—ALBERT SCHWEITZER

CONTENTS

*Max could carry three
tennis balls in his mouth.*

Until one has loved an animal,
a part of one's soul remains unawakened.
—ANATOLE FRANCE

❋

THE BEGINNING
Someday

I was nearly thirty years old before I had a dog of my own. My sister Alice always had dogs, and I learned to love them through her. But my own living situation did not allow for a dog until I moved to Oregon and married. My husband, Jon, brought home a golden retriever puppy. His fur was like goose down. When he yawned, his pink tongue curled up and he smelled sweetly of puppy breath. When I held him, he kissed my neck, then buried his nose in the crook of my arm. Jon had rescued him from a college-bound girl; she had purchased him on a whim in a pet store. Of course, the dorm did not allow pets. And of course, I could not resist him.

We named him Max.

I wanted Max to be my walking buddy, but he pulled me down the road. Full grown, he weighed sixty pounds. I called a friend, a longtime dog owner, for advice. She suggested we meet at a park. I got there early and sat down on a bench to wait. Max lay at my feet, as I held his leash. My friend arrived a few minutes later, walking up behind us. Max immediately scrambled under me toward her, yanking me to the ground with a *thump*. He pulled me halfway under the bench before I let go of his leash. Embarrassed, I crawled out from beneath the bench, while Max cavorted around her.

"Looks like you need some help," she said wryly, as she extended a hand. "Let's start with how to control Max." And my learning began.

Max taught me a lot about raising and training a dog—mostly what *not* to do. In fact, I'm sure I made every mistake possible on him. But he still loved me, and I loved him. He could carry three tennis balls in his mouth at one time; it never failed to make me laugh. On cold evenings, we'd cuddle in front of the woodstove.

Max was not a healthy dog. We learned later he came from a puppy mill; he was bred solely for the wholesale pet trade. He lived less than five years. When it became apparent that he could not live without extraordinary medical measures, Jon and I decided to humanely end his suffering.

The night before the vet appointment, I sat with Max. His once-downy coat was now lumpy and dry. He was bald in some spots. His skin had basically stopped functioning. But he still knew how to lick my neck and nuzzle into my arms. He sensed that I was upset, and he tried to make me feel better with his kisses. I could barely stand it. Max was comforting *me* for making the decision to put *him* to sleep.

The next morning, I told Jon, "I can't go with you. I just can't do it." So Jon took Max. He was the one who held Max as Dr. Ross first administered a sedative that would relax him. Several minutes later, Dr. Ross gently injected a second needle. Jon slowly stroked Max's ears and whispered to him, "You're a good dog, a good boy," and Max quietly slipped from this world to the next.

Now, I regret that I did not go. Max had asked nothing from me but love, and I gave it. With love comes responsibility; I had failed in my responsibility to him.

Months passed. Max's empty bed was a constant reminder of the empty spot in our lives. Jon wanted to get another golden retriever. I wanted a black Labrador. I figured the wash-and-wear coat of a Lab was better suited to our country setting. Jon and I normally can discuss matters logically and come to a common decision, but on this matter, neither one of us would give in, so we did nothing.

On a Saturday afternoon in June, we went grocery shopping together. Well, actually, I got the groceries, while Jon read car magazines. I met him outside the store.

"Come with me," he said mysteriously as he steered my cart to a truck parked two rows away. In the back, a litter of puppies romped. Some were black; some were gold. The sign read "Puppies: Half Golden Retriever/Half Black Lab — $20." Only one was left unclaimed.

We had our dog.

With our fifteen acres on the river, I knew this pup would live "The Life of Riley," so that's what we called him: Riley. He had black Lab hair, but the bone structure of a golden.

I liked that he was a hybrid. That meant he probably would not suffer from the inbreeding problems that had plagued Max. I liked that he had lived his first nine weeks in the home of a busy family. He had been very well socialized. And I hoped that his mom would now be spayed. I knew Riley and his littermates were lucky to find homes; many do not.

I was determined to do much better by Riley than I had by Max. Dogs trained to guide the blind had intrigued me since I read a book about them as a child.

Someday, I will get involved in that program, I said to myself.

For now, I studied the basic guide-dog training techniques and applied as many as I could to Riley. We attended obedience classes. The result was a well-behaved, loving companion.

I learned that Guide Dogs for the Blind, based in San Rafael, California, was even using the Lab-golden cross in its program. I'd look at

Riley and wonder if he could have been a guide dog.

Once again I thought, *Someday I should get involved in that program.*

A few years later, my mother died. As anyone who has lost a parent knows, it's an event that places you squarely in front of your own mortality. You find yourself reviewing your "Life's To Do" list. On my list was the guide-dog program. It was probably Mom who had given me the book about the program. Mom taught me by example about giving something back.

Someday has arrived, I thought.

I drove three hours north to tour the Oregon campus of Guide Dogs for the Blind. The spotless kennels, vet clinic, dormitory, and other buildings sit nestled among towering fir trees in a rural area east of Portland. I watched trainers patiently and lovingly working with young golden retrievers, Labradors, and German shepherds. I wanted to help.

My enthusiasm spilled over to others in our community, and we formed a puppy-raising club. Our job is to take puppies from Guide Dogs' breeding program and raise them for about a year as members of our families. We teach them basic obedience and good house manners and socialize them by taking them to public places. Riley has accepted the guide pups in our home with the tolerance of a big brother.

The guide-dog program has further opened me to the magic our canine friends can work. I started to volunteer at our local animal shelter, to take dogs into nursing homes, and to help with pet adoptions.

Over the years, I have met hundreds of dogs. Guide pups. Working guides. Adopted-from-the-shelter mutts. Each one has changed someone's life. Every dog has a story. Now, *someday* has arrived for writing down some of those stories. ❖

*When Kilroy saw
her, he smiled.*

Dogs know exactly what makes them happy—
doing something for someone.
They will do everything they can think of
to please their human companion,
and any signs that they have been successful
make them very happy.
—JOHN RICHARD STEPHENS

❧

KILROY AND ALICE

"Kilroy is going to make it," Terri Jo said. I knew just what she was talking about. As a Guide Dogs for the Blind puppy-raising leader in southern Oregon, I had worked with dogs who seemed destined to become a guide for a visually impaired person.

Confident. Bright. Loving. Kilroy, a yellow Lab, had it all.

As a puppy-raising leader in eastern Oregon, Terri Jo had watched him grow from a nine-week-old ball of fluff to a handsome, mature dog—ready for formal training at the guide-dog campus.

His raisers, the Miller family, had taught him basic obedience and had socialized him by taking him to public places, including high school every day with the daughters.

"The kids love him," Terri Jo said. "We've had lots of dogs in our group. Kilroy is one of our best."

I met Kilroy through my sister Alice, a dog lover from way back. When Alice was a single woman, Lucy, her female yellow Lab mix, had been her constant companion for thirteen years. Alice held Lucy in her arms when the time came for the vet to relieve her suffering. Even today, Alice still chokes up a bit when she talks about Lucy.

Alice works as a reading teacher with special-needs kids. She connects easily with the children. They love her.

Recently, Alice became a single woman again after nearly eighteen years of marriage. It's been a very difficult and fearful time for her. The emotional devastation, financial worries, safety concerns, and loneliness overwhelm her at times.

She set up a new home in a duplex, much smaller than the four-bedroom home she left behind. She also left behind the family dog. Alice has hung pictures, arranged furniture, and made a home for herself and her teenaged children, Shane and Tessa.

"But the house still feels empty," she said to me. "I miss having a dog."

She was spending a few days with me—a short respite from all the stress. We took long walks and shared sister-talk late into the night.

I had a guide pup in my home that weekend. Alice fed him, groomed him, and loved him. She sat on the floor and gave him an all-over body massage. The pup stretched and let out a long, contented sigh. Alice sighed, too.

"We've got to get you a dog, Alice," I said. She nodded.

I knew a dog could do even more than provide companionship for Alice. Getting a dog is one of the best actions a single woman can take for personal safety. The simple bark of a dog is a great deterrent to anyone who is up to no good. Alice walks four miles a day. Many evenings, she's alone in the house. She needed a dog.

I put the word out. I called other guide-dog leaders and raisers I knew. Alice filled out an application to adopt a guide-pup dropout or, rather, a "career-changed" pup as the organization prefers to describe them.

Several months passed. Then came a flurry of phone calls, starting with a call from the Guide Dogs career-change department. Kilroy was being released from the program. He had completed two-thirds of the formal training but occasionally "marked," or urinated, when working in harness—unacceptable for a guide dog, but not a problem for a pet. The Miller family planned to raise another pup, so they decided not to adopt him. Guide Dogs would place him with someone on its waiting list for career-changed dogs.

When no one answered at Alice's house, the representative called me. "Is Alice interested in Kilroy?" she asked.

"You bet," I replied.

Next, I called Terri Jo to learn more about Kilroy. I could hear the disappointment in her voice. "I really thought Kilroy was going to make it," she said.

The next day, Alice, Tessa, and I drove to the guide-dog training campus and waited for Kilroy in the kennel kitchen. About one hundred freshly washed, stainless-steel food bowls stood neatly stacked against one wall. Barrels of dog food filled an adjoining alcove. A large tabby cat slept contentedly atop one of the file cabinets at the back of the room. He awoke and blinked sleepily, then tucked his nose back into his tail, ignoring us.

An instructor's assistant brought Kilroy in. He stood for a moment in the doorway—motionless, alert, taking in the situation.

Alice knelt down and called him. When Kilroy saw her, he smiled and came to her exuberantly. He licked her face. Maybe he liked the smell of her skin or the taste of her tears, but he licked her again. Tessa hugged him.

After the paperwork was complete, we left the kennel kitchen. Three trainers were working with several adult Labradors in the patio. Kilroy, between Alice and Tessa, walked confidently past them. I unlatched the gate, and the three of them passed through. I looked back at the dogs in training, at the life Kilroy was leaving. Kilroy only looked forward to the life ahead.

To Terri Jo and the Miller family, I say, "Kilroy *did* make it. He's already made a difference. Thank you." ❖

*Going fishin'
with Dad.*

August 28

Dear Kilroy,

Welcome to the family. My name is Riley. Since my mom and your mom are sisters, that means we're cousins. I'm half black Labrador and half golden retriever. Mom and Dad picked me out of a box in a pickup truck at the grocery store. Everyone says I look like a very big black Lab, but if you rub the top of my head you can feel the golden retriever "bump." Mom calls it my "intelligence bump." Dad just calls me "Knothead."

Things I like to do: eat, go for walks with Mom, eat, go fishing with Dad, swim, fetch my Frisbee, eat.

Anyway, I'm now ten years old. So, if you need any advice about being a pet, drop me a line.

Love,

Riley

✺

August 30

Dear Riley,

Thank you for the family welcome. Can't wait to meet you. I hear you are a wonderful pet. Your dad calls you "Knothead"? My new mom calls me "Knucklehead" sometimes, but always affectionately. I've learned a lot about being a guide dog. I'm just not sure how to be a pet. I'm glad I can count on you for advice.

I'm getting settled into my new home. Sometimes, when Mom hears a car slow down outside, she peeks through the front curtains. Then she checks the locks on the doors.

She doesn't sleep very well, either. She made me a soft bed right next to hers. Every time she stirs, I get up and put my head on the edge of the bed to see if she needs me. I don't understand why she cries, but I think she likes my cold, wet nose on her cheek, because she says, "Oh, Kilroy!" and gently strokes my ears.

After she falls back to sleep, I curl up on my blanket and listen to her steady breathing. I like that.

Love,

Kilroy

✺

September 1

Dear Kilroy,

    Just be there. Love her. That's what she needs.

Love,

Riley

✺

September 5

Dear Riley,

Is it okay for pets to drag flower pots around the patio?
Love,
Kilroy

✷

September 6

Dear Kilroy,
    No.
Love,
Riley

*The loss of his eye was
neither good nor bad.
It just was.*

My goal in life is to become
as good a person as my dog thinks I am.

—ANONYMOUS

❊

RILEY'S EYE

Riley has only one eye. He wasn't born that way. He lost it when he was five.

I first noticed a problem when he was sitting in front of me. Even when he sits, he looms large. Riley weighs nearly ninety pounds, but he's sleek and tall. His head reaches about level with my chest if I'm in a chair. I was sitting in the kitchen, stroking his head hard. He loves it. I use both hands to smooth back his face, pull his skin taut over his eyes, then skim over his ears. I usually scratch a little behind his ears, too, and he grunts in satisfaction. That day, as I was stroking him, I noticed that his right eye appeared grayer than his left. Yes, it definitely was different.

A few days later, our vet peered into the eye with a scope. "I see some sort of mass," Dr. Ross said, his face betraying his worry.

We took Riley to a pet ophthalmologist, who confirmed Dr. Ross's diagnosis. A tumor was growing inside Riley's right eye. She recommended removal of the eyeball and tear ducts. I blanched at the thought, but then realized the loss of an eye was minor. If it were a malignant tumor, it could jeopardize Riley's life. In humans, eye cancer is almost always fatal.

A week later, Dr. Ross performed the surgery, and a biopsy brought good news. The mass was not malignant.

But poor Riley! The right side of his face was completely shaved, revealing pale white skin, a stark contrast to the shiny black fur that covers him. Ugly, dark stitches now closed the sunken socket where his eye had been. He looked awful.

Jon and I fretted over him. Imagine how we'd feel if this happened to us, we'd say to each other.

How could I look in the mirror? I thought. *What would other people think about how I looked?*

But Riley didn't care. Except for a little soreness (he recoiled once when he bumped his head against my leg), he was fine. He hadn't changed at all.

He still bounced joyfully whenever I got out his leash. He still made happy yodel-yawns as I dished up his dinner. He still plopped his head in my lap when I sat on the floor with him.

None of his dog friends noticed. Not one made a comment about how funny he looked. Not one looked away in embarrassment or disgust. He was the same ol' Riley.

For Riley, the loss of his eye was neither good nor bad. It just was.

Maybe we love our canine friends so much because they naturally possess traits that we'd like to see more of in ourselves. They accept adversity without question. They accept each other—and us—without judging. They love us unconditionally, no matter what we look like.

Nowadays, most people hardly notice Riley's missing eye. Once his hair grew back, the hollow socket seemed to disappear. At times, I can't remember which eye is gone until I look at him. Then I stroke his head in the way he loves: smoothing his face, scratching his ears.

If I catch myself being judgmental, I think about Riley's eye. Even with just one eye, he can see the world more clearly than a lot of humans. ❖

✺

October 30

Dear Kilroy,

I have a new sister, a yellow Lab. Her name is Saffron. She's your cousin, too, and not just because she's my sister. Mom found out that you two have the same grandfather. Mom takes her out a lot. They go shopping together and to movies. Saffron has to wear a green Guide Dog in Training jacket whenever she goes out. The other night they went to a nursing home and visited the people who live there. I'm a little jealous, but Mom gives me extra hugs and tells me I'm still her fluffy bunny-boo.

Love,

Riley

※

November 4

Dear Riley,

Don't worry, your mom loves you more than any other dog in the whole world. She told me.

I remember when I always wore my green jacket. I went to high school every day and to basketball games and to aerobics class. The grocery store was my favorite, especially the meat department.

Later, I went away to another school and lived with a lot of other happy dogs. Every day we got to go more places and learn new stuff.

After Mom adopted me, I never wore my green jacket again, and now I don't go inside all those neat places anymore. Oh well, giving up my jacket for Mom was a very good trade.

Love,

Kilroy

Twenty chain-link runs . . .
each one contained
a dog in need of a home.

Perhaps nothing can wrench the heart of a dog lover more
than the pitiful, hardly daring-to-be-hopeful gaze
of an abandoned dog waiting to be adopted.

—JOHN GALSWORTHY

❋

RENEE AND LACEY

The first thing you notice about my friend Renee is her hair. Tight strawberry-golden curls cascade around her face and neck. The next thing you notice is her laugh. She shares it freely and often. Deep-throated and generous.

A talented graphic designer, Renee works at a printing company. I drop by several times a week to discuss projects. Renee has three fair-haired little girls, a handsome husband, and a house with a picket fence. Her favorite color is purple. Occasionally, she dog-sits Riley. The whole family fell in love with Riley the first time he stayed with them, and they decided they wanted a dog of their own.

"Can you help us?" Renee asked me one day, when I stopped by to examine some printing proofs. I had Saffron in tow, my new guide pup in training.

"Of course," I replied.

My involvement in raising guide dogs is well known in our small community. Public service announcements regularly broadcast my name and telephone number. Every few days I get a dog-related call, and not all of them are guide-dog specific. One morning, a call came in about a black Labrador at the county animal shelter.

"Do you know anyone who wants a pet?" the caller asked. I thought of Renee.

During lunch, Renee and I drove up to the shelter. The barking of too many dogs greeted us as we pulled into the parking lot. Inwardly, I cringed as we walked down the concrete aisle dividing about twenty chain-link runs. Each one contained a dog in need of a home. I felt anger at the people who had abandoned these dogs. Some were strays; others were castoffs, their owners tired of them for whatever reason.

About 2.5 million dogs are left at animal shelters each year, according to the American Society for the Prevention of Cruelty to Animals. Sixty percent are euthanized (yes, killed) simply because there are not enough homes. That's 1.5 million death sentences every year—more than 4,000 every day. Those numbers could be drastically reduced if dog owners would neuter and spay their pets. Guide Dogs for the Blind always fixes working guides and career-change pups; only a select few remain intact for its breeding program.

The black Lab was lying in the corner of the last run on the left. A golden retriever in the next kennel wiggled happily as we walked by. The Lab eyed us suspiciously. Her collar was too tight and dug into her neck. I loosened it a notch and attached a leash. Outside, she sniffed at the grass, paying no attention to us. She was massive, with a gray-flecked coat; her jaw was wide and muscular. "I don't think she's all Lab," I said to Renee.

Renee furrowed her brow as she watched me work with the dog. I felt like I was walking a bulldozer or, rather, it was walking me. "She's not for you," I said.

A look of relief crossed Renee's face. "Let's look at the golden retriever," I added. Back we went.

The kennel attendants said the golden had been picked up off the streets—no collar, no calls from a distressed owner. She'd been at the shelter for more than a week. Her allotted time was almost up.

When I slipped the leash over her head, I noticed she smelled rank, the smell of being in a kennel too long. Her long hair was matted. But when we took her outside, she pranced and danced. A gentle tug on the leash brought her right back to my side.

Renee smiled and stroked the dog's head. The golden promptly nuzzled her hand.

"Wonder how she'd be with kids," she said. As if on cue, a young couple with a small child walked up from a car. The little boy squealed and threw his arms around the dog. I firmly held the leash, prepared to pull back if she made any aggressive moves. But the golden retriever sat calmly, soaking in the child's affection.

The parents looked at us. "Is this dog available?" the mother asked.

"Sorry, she's mine!" Renee said with a grin.

I like to think that the black Lab found a home, but I'm thankful for the call that took us to the shelter that day. Renee and I agree that the little golden was just waiting for Renee to come for her.

After a full family conference, they decided to call her "Lacey," mainly because it was the only suggested name that their two-year-old daughter could pronounce.

Last week, I stopped by Renee's house. A dog dish has been added to the colorful chaos of toys corralled by the picket fence. As I let myself in the back door, a beautifully groomed Lacey bounded up to greet me. She smelled faintly of peach shampoo. Happy laughter drifted up from the basement.

"We're down here," came Renee's voice. Lacey led me down the stairs, her purple collar peeking out from the strawberry-golden curls around her neck. ❖

※

November 20

Dear Riley,

Mom has a new job. I think she likes it, because she's singing a lot lately. I get to go with her a couple times a week. It's a big university. At lunch time, she walks me around campus. I love the path that passes the cow barns. It smells absolutely out of this world.

Yesterday on our walk, I met Tierney. Sigh. She's a yellow Lab guide pup. She lives with a woman who works in the home economics department.

Sigh . . . she has a wonderful smile.

I wanted Tierney to notice me, so I started showing off how well I can "talk." I said "ah-woooooo, woooo woooo woo" and wiggled my butt.

Oh Tierney, you have such pretty brown eyes.

Riley, have you ever been in love?

Love,

Kilroy

※

November 22

Dear Kilroy,

Forget her. There's nothing you can do about it anyway.

Love,

Riley

※

November 25

Dear Kilroy,

The Four Footed Freedom Club (we raise guide-dog puppies) would love to have you and your mom join us in the Corvallis Community Parade on Friday, December 12. We will meet between 6:30 and 6:45 P.M. on Washington Street, between Sixth and Seventh streets (south side). We are entry number 29. The theme is "Nutcracker Fantasy." Please wear lights, antlers, bells, or anything festive. If you have any questions, give me a call.

Sincerely,

Alice Mills Morrow and Tierney, the Guide Pup

Please wear lights,
antlers, bells, or
anything festive.

✺

November 27

Dear Ms. Morrow:

Thank you very much for the invitation to the holiday parade. Unfortunately, Mom and I will be out of town. I am very sorry to miss the parade and even more sorry to miss seeing Tierney again.

Mom and I marched in a parade last summer with the guide-dog group in Roseburg. We had a great time. There were fire engines, a band, some horses, popcorn, and lots of people. I got to walk with other career-change guide dogs, behind all the young pups in training. We looked pretty good, if I do say so myself. Of course, dodging all the horse piles was a little tricky, so be careful.

Thanks again,

Kilroy

*Lucy bolted, and her leash
slipped from my hands.*

> *I never met a dog*
> *who didn't like to make people laugh.*
> —CAROL LEA BENJAMIN

※

BIG SISTER

There is a photo of Alice and me in our family album, taken when I was about one year old. Alice was seven or eight. I'm sitting in a baby chair under a tree; she's kneeling next to me, teaching me how to clap. The camera caught us in mid-clap. Our hands are frozen about an inch apart. I'm giggling and looking up at her adoringly. Alice is grinning. Her hair is cut short, pixie style. Summer freckles spread across her tanned face. We're wearing sleeveless, striped, matching sunsuits. The black and-white photo doesn't reveal the color, but I think they were yellow and blue. Later, I probably wore her sunsuit as a hand-me-down.

When I was nine, the age difference did not work in our favor. She was sixteen and wanted nothing to do with a scrawny, goofy little sister. She and our next-door neighbor, also sixteen, retreated into her bedroom, slamming the door to keep me out.

When I was thirteen, our relationship changed again. Alice and the next-door neighbor had their own place—a tiny bungalow at the beach, about an hour's drive from our suburban Los Angeles tract home. Now, Alice liked me and would invite me down for the weekend. I felt so grown up when I visited her. We'd talk late into the night. I slept on her living-room floor in a sleeping bag with her yellow Lab mix, Lucy, curled up at my feet.

The year before, Alice had adopted Lucy from the animal shelter. As a puppy, Lucy looked mostly like her yellow Labrador mother, but as she grew, her Great Dane heritage started to show, too. She was tall and slender, gentle and sweet. I welcomed her body warmth as we slept on the floor. Nights at the beach can be cool with fog and sea breezes.

Alice had a new boyfriend that summer. He had a younger brother, a year older than I was. I thought he was the cutest boy I had ever met. We spent days playing ping-pong at the community rec center. On the last day of my visit for the summer, we walked to the beach. It was nearly sunset; the lifeguards and most of the day crowd had left. We sat down in the still-warm sand and leaned against guard tower 23. He took my hand. No boy had ever held my hand before. My heart nearly stopped beating. I felt embarrassed, elated, overwhelmed—and I couldn't think of a thing to say.

So we sat in silence, holding hands, and watching the sun disappear into the Pacific. My hand became sweaty, but for the life of me I would not move it. That was all: just two sweaty hands and a sunset. Nothing more. I was in love.

That night, during our late-night talk, I told Alice. She hugged me as only a big sister could. Lucy stuck her cold nose up between us, trying to get in on the hug. We laughed and wrapped our arms around Lucy, too.

School started, and I received a letter from him. He invited me to Disneyland.

"You're too young to go on a date," Mom said matter-of-factly when I told her. So I tucked the letter away in my special shoebox with my other treasures. No more letters arrived. Sometimes when I felt gawky and unattractive, I'd pull out the letter and read it again. Soon, I had it memorized.

Two years later, our high school basketball team was scheduled to play his team on our home court. I knew he played basketball; I had seen his name in the box scores of our local newspaper. For two weeks I scoured my closet, trying to decide what to wear. I settled on a pink-striped shirt and blue jeans.

I arrived at the gym in time to watch warm-ups. I recognized him immediately, even though he was much taller now. It was a hard, physical game. When he rested on the bench, I thought I saw him scanning the crowd. I don't remember who won. At the final buzzer, I pushed my way through the crowd to the gym floor and called out to him. He didn't hear me, so I yelled his name again. I was afraid he'd disappear into the locker room. This time, he turned around.

"Over here!" I called again.

When he saw me his face split into a grin. The rest of the team shoved by him as he stood rooted to the wooden floor. He walked back to me at half court, wiping the sweat from his face with a towel.

"I didn't know you were here," he said. His voice was an octave lower than what I remembered.

"I wouldn't have missed it for anything," I replied. There was so much I wanted to say but couldn't. *Ask me for my phone number,* I thought.

He glanced to his team's sidelines. A girl stood there watching us. She held a boy's letterman's jacket in her arms. In an instant I understood. I felt my face get hot. I mumbled good-bye and walked away.

At home, Alice was finishing up her laundry. I asked Mom if I could go back with Alice to her house. I grabbed my sleeping bag and an overnight case, and I helped load her Volkswagen. On the drive, I told her everything. Lucy sat on the floor in the back, but poked her head between us. Alice asked a few questions; mostly she listened.

Lucy put her head in my lap. It was late when we got to Alice's house.

"Will you take Lucy out in the morning?" Alice asked me before we went to bed. "I want to sleep in."

"Sure," I said as I rolled out my sleeping bag.

It was sunup when I awoke. Lucy had moved from her normal position at my feet and lay curled up next to my side. She stretched and shook. I pulled on my jeans and my favorite red, hooded sweatshirt. I hooked a leash to Lucy, and we let ourselves out quietly. In my mind, I already saw myself sitting on the beach, at lifeguard tower 23. I'd gaze dramatically to the ocean, reliving first love. I was sure I would cry.

But Lucy had a different idea. As soon as her paws hit the beach, the stimulation of the foggy ocean air and the cool sand overwhelmed her puppy-heightened senses. She tucked her tail and started running in tight circles around me. She ran so fast that her back legs skidded out from beneath her. When she saw a flock of seagulls, she bolted, and her leash slipped from my hands. I ran after her as she headed for the water. She chased a wave, and it receded back to the sea. She looked triumphant, only to find another wave coming in at full speed. She bit at it, but when it refused to stop, she turned and scampered away. Now a sand crab caught her attention, and she pursued it until it disappeared down a hole. She dug frantically, spraying me with sand

and bits of seaweed. I grabbed the leash and plopped down next to her. I was exhausted from trying to catch her—and from laughing.

Alice was up and dressed when we got back. It occurred to me that she had asked me to take Lucy out not because she wanted to sleep in, but because she knew I needed Lucy's laughter. A decade later, when Alice called to tell me about Lucy's paralysis and the decision to put her to sleep, I remembered our morning on the beach when Lucy ran so freely and joyfully. Why can't dogs live longer? Their life span should match ours. Since it doesn't, we are destined to say too many good-byes.

Lucy taught me well. Many years later, when the time came for me to be the "big sister"—when Alice came to my house as her marriage crumbled—I recalled the lesson of laughter.

Jon went to bed, as Alice and I stayed up late, talking. She needed to talk and to cry, but she also needed to laugh. Before we turned in, I asked her to take Riley out in the morning. I suggested the wildlife preserve across the road—sixteen square miles of rolling hills, creeks, pines, and oak trees.

At sunup I heard the back door open and close. I lay in bed recalling a long-ago summer, a beach sunset, a tiny bungalow, and Lucy's angelic face.

It was February, and the early morning temperature hovered near freezing. I got up, built a fire in the woodstove, and made coffee. When I saw two figures, one human and one canine, cresting our driveway, I put on my down jacket and walked out to meet them.

I'm not sure what happened on the walk, but Riley was panting hard and Alice was smiling broadly. I hugged her. Riley leaned heavily against our legs, trying be a part of the "sister" moment. We laughed. Our breath hung in the air, and the bare tree branches sparkled in frost.

I think Alice and I would be friends even if we weren't sisters. Our love runs deep and strong. We made very different life choices, and we avoid talking politics. But we laugh a lot when we're together. We have fun. We share a lifetime of experiences. She was the one who taught me, through Lucy, about the healing power of dogs. We listen when the other needs to talk. We ease each other's disappointments in life and love. She applauds my successes, and I do the same for her. After all, she was also the one who taught me how to clap. ❖

✺

January 15

Dear Mr. [name withheld]:

Recently, I visited your restaurant with Saffron, my guide dog in training. One of your employees asked us to leave even though Saffron was wearing her green Guide Dog Puppy jacket. The Americans with Disabilities Act allows service dogs access to all public places. Access for service dogs in training vary by state, but Oregon law gives them the same rights as service dogs. Refusing access is a Class C misdemeanor with a $200 penalty. Even though Oregon law allowed us to be in your restaurant, we left. We do not want to be where we are not welcome. We do, however, want to educate the public about the legal rights of the blind and guide dogs. Thus, I am enclosing some literature about guide dogs and a copy of the Oregon law. Your restaurant provides great opportunities for training, including interesting smells, people, and noise. It is critical for the pups to receive exposure to such places if they are to be successful later as guides. We will not return if that is your wish, but I am hopeful that the next time a guide pup in training visits your restaurant, she will be welcomed.

Sincerely,

Nora Vitz Harrison

※

January 19

Dear Mr. [name withheld]:

Thank you very much for your kind reply and invitation to return to your restaurant with Saffron. The gift certificates are much appreciated.

Sincerely,

Nora Vitz Harrison

*Nash, a svelte, male
yellow Lab puppy.*

A well-trained dog will make
no attempt to share your lunch.
He will just make you feel so guilty
that you cannot enjoy it.
—HELEN THOMSON

❊

NO EXPERIENCE NECESSARY

$\mathcal{W}$hen I interview prospective raisers of guide-dog puppies, I always warn them that they can forget about being anonymous. Walking into a grocery store with a good-looking, well-behaved pup in a green jacket always attracts attention.

"Be prepared to be noticed," I tell them. And plan extra time to do errands. The pup won't slow you down, but the questions of interested strangers will:

"Don't you get attached to your pup?"

"How can you give him up?"

The answers are: "Of course we get attached. We wouldn't be doing a good job if we didn't fall in love with our pups. And we can give them up because we know someone else needs them more than we do."

"Do you have a lot of experience training dogs?" is another question we hear often.

Our puppy-raising group was pathetically lacking in dog-training experience when we started, but we made up for it in enthusiasm. The very first puppy delivered to our group was placed in the arms of Sherry, a self-avowed cat lover. Sherry had never had a dog.

But she applied herself with determination. She studied the puppy-training manual, viewed the instructional videos, and purchased the necessary supplies. She gained approval from her employer, a local printer, to take the pup with her to work every day.

Sherry received Nash, a svelte, male yellow Lab puppy, on a Tuesday. Forty-eight hours later, we had a meeting with Pat, our Guide Dogs adviser. Sherry was the last to arrive. Nash waddled in behind her. He looked like an overblown, fuzzy beach ball with four little sticks for legs.

"Good grief, Sherry, how much are you feeding him?" I exclaimed.

"Three cups—like the feeding instructions say," Sherry replied a bit defensively.

"Just three?" Pat asked incredulously.

"Yes. Three cups, three times a day."

We burst into laughter. Sherry had unwittingly tripled Nash's feeding amounts. It was supposed to be three cups a day—*total*. Fortunately, Sherry has a sense of humor and laughed along with us when she realized her mistake.

Several months later, it was Nash who showed me just how *"un* anonymous" a person can be with a guide pup. In our club, we share and trade pups. It gives them a variety of experiences and teaches them that they must behave for everyone—not just their primary raiser.

I asked Sherry if I could take Nash with me to a community-theater production. Alice had one of the leading roles. Since I was new at this, we arrived early. Nash fit nicely under my chair and promptly fell asleep.

This is going to be easy, I thought. *No one even knows he's here.*

The auditorium filled, and the lights dimmed. Sometime during the third scene, as the hero was about to kiss the heroine, Nash let out a long, very loud, sleepy groan. The woman next to me tittered. The man in front of me shifted in his seat and glanced backwards. I slunk down in my seat.

But Nash wasn't done yet. No more sounds came from him, but slowly I became aware of the very distinct odor of doggie gas. It was emanating upward from beneath my seat, strong and pungent, and spreading at least three rows in every direction. My eyes watered. I coughed discreetly.

As the lights came up for intermission, Nash awoke. He stood and looked around sleepily. The man in front of me also stood, stretched, and nonchalantly glanced back at me. Then he saw Nash.

"It's a dog!" he said to me, stating the obvious. "I thought it was *you*." Realizing what he had said, the man turned crimson, but I took no offense and in fact was chuckling with the others around us.

The constant attention a guide pup brings can be hard on inexperienced raisers—especially the shy, young ones. But it also can have a very positive effect on them.

When I interviewed Susan and her daughter Michelle, I concluded that Susan would be a terrific raiser. She had experience and a real love for dogs. I wasn't so sure about fourteen-year-old Michelle. She barely participated in the interview. I interpreted her quiet nature as lack of interest.

How wrong I was.

When I was unable to accommodate a speaking request at a local elementary school, I asked Michelle to do it. She was reluctant at first, but finally agreed. I was surprised and delighted when Michelle called me after the event. She gushed about how much fun it had been. Her pup, a female Lab named Silky, wowed the children.

"And I talked for twenty minutes and answered all their questions," Michelle said, hardly able to contain her excitement.

About a year later, Silky graduated as a guide dog. Michelle, composed and confident, gave a short speech and handed over Silky's leash to her new eighty-year-old visually impaired partner in a ceremony before three hundred people. Michelle is now raising her fourth guide pup.

Despite our early inexperience, the three puppies who launched our group got off to a good start. One pup became a guide for a woman in Utah. Another became a guide in Arizona.

Sherry's pup, Nash, completed all his formal training. One week before graduation, his blind partner decided Nash was not quite the right match for him. It's critical that the blind partner have complete confidence in the dog; the instructors work hard to make good matches based on temperament, pace, size, and personality. But sometimes it doesn't work out. When a second match failed, Nash came back to Sherry as a pet.

Today, he serves as the official greeter in the printing business where he was raised. Each time the front door opens, Nash lazily strolls out from beneath Sherry's desk to say hello. At home, he coexists peacefully with Sherry's cats. Meanwhile, Sherry has helped raise many more guide pups, and several have become working guides.

Do you need training experience to raise a guide pup? No. You need love, time, and a commitment to do your best.

A sense of humor also helps. ❖

❋

March 2

Dear Riley,

Well, yesterday I failed miserably at being a responsible pet. I have no idea what caused me to attack the phone box on the side of the house, but I did. When Mom came home and tried to use the phone, it didn't work. She checked the other phones and then went outside. There, dangling from the wall by frayed wires, was the phone box. My chewing had left teeth marks all over the plastic cover. Boy oh boy, was Mom upset. I didn't mean to cause so much damage.

Today after the repairman left, I decided to taste the new plastic box. Unfortunately, Mom was waiting for me. As I started to take a nip from the corner of the box, she leaped out of her hiding place behind the door, yelled "NO!" and pulled sharply on my collar. It scared the tar out of me. I about jumped out of my fur. She let me walk near the box again, but I wouldn't touch it. No sir-eeee. Then, she took me inside. I was so upset that I went straight to my bed and stayed there for two hours. Finally, Mom came looking for me. She lay down on the floor next to me and put her head on my shoulder. After she stroked my head for a long time, I felt better. So did she.

Love,

Kilroy

March 5

Dear Kilroy,

Our picnic table benches have gnawed-off corners. I'm ashamed to say, I did that in my youth. Learn from this experience. You will be a better pet for it.

Love,

Riley

*In the afternoons, she lies
on the front porch mat.*

> *[Concern for animals] is a matter of taking*
> *the side of the weak against the strong,*
> *something the best people have always done.*
> —HARRIET BEECHER STOWE

✻

GRACE

The Douglas County animal shelter sits on a five-acre knoll a mile off Interstate 5—not much else around except for the huge log yard next door. Southern Oregon is timber country, and a log yard is just as its name implies: acres of log piles the size of warehouse buildings. Trucks deliver the logs; cranes lift and stack them; sprinklers keep them wet so they don't dry out before they can be milled. The logs hide the shelter building until you round the curve, climb the hill, and pass the gates into the parking lot. Oak trees provide some shade around the building. Wild grasses and weeds provide the landscaping.

The only human neighbor lives about a half mile away. Good thing. Even the most dog-loving person would not want to live too close to forty barking dogs in concrete kennels. The noise can be deafening, especially when every run is full, and they usually are. Long ago, the number of abandoned and stray dogs and cats swamped the number of kennels and cages. The squatty, overcrowded building is cinder block with a concrete floor. Concrete is good for a kennel because it can be hosed down. But this concrete is old and cracked.

The first time I saw the shelter, the paint was peeling from the wooden windows and trim. The finicky plumbing sporadically backed up and refused to accept anything more down its drains. The exercise yard fence had holes in it, and the latch on the gate didn't work. Even the soap dispenser in the tiny restroom was broken. It was as if the whole building had given up. It had been built in the 1950s by volunteers. In the '60s, our county government took it over; through the years, attempts at creative management bogged down. Oh, it poked along, providing the services required by law, but not much beyond that—until a new sheriff came to town.

He really wasn't new to our area, but that phrase has a certain ring of change to it. Sheriff Main had spent more than fifteen years as a county deputy, plus many years in private business. He's a compassionate man, who has adopted two dogs and a cat from the shelter. He's committed to making things work. He started asking questions as soon as he was elected. Responsibility for the shelter had been shuffled from county department to county department for years.

Sheriff Main had the good sense to ask "Why?" and "How can we do it better?" He also had the good sense to call Cheryl, the president of our local Humane Society.

Cheryl is a bit eccentric, which makes her interesting and fun. She's been known to plant radishes in her garden while wearing pajamas. Cheryl speaks her mind freely, loudly, and often, especially if the topic is animals. She's the first to admit she sometimes talks too much, but her words rise from a passion within. She personally pays vet bills for the needy. She will take on anyone or any organization in defense of the defenseless. She is known throughout the state for her good works. She believes in destiny and jokingly says God calls her daily with His plan for her.

The sheriff suggested to Cheryl that animal welfare would be better served if a private organization ran the shelter. The county would contract with the organization, thus providing dependable funding to the new entity. The private group would be able to qualify for grants and other funding that the county could not.

"Will you help me make it happen?" he asked her.

She hesitated and said she'd think about it. It was December, a couple weeks before Christmas, a busy time of year.

A few days later, Cheryl received another call, seemingly unrelated to the sheriff's request. It was not God calling, "but then again, maybe it was," she says now with a small, knowing smile. It had to do with a female retriever. The dog's name was Bitsy, a silly name for a large, yellow Lab, but that was the name on the accompanying paperwork when her owner dropped her off at the animal shelter in Salem, a couple hours north of our town.

Bitsy had lived her life in a cage, producing puppies. In four years, she had had six litters as part of a puppy mill. That's what it's called when dogs are mass produced for the wholesale pet trade. *Life* magazine in 1966 wrote an exposé on puppy mills entitled "Concentration Camps for Dogs"; the haunting images helped launch a movement to curtail such operations. But puppy mills still exist.

Bitsy's owner was a college student who was financing his education by selling her puppies. He used her up—when she could no longer produce puppies, he dumped her at the shelter.

Her nose was bloody and raw from rubbing it against the chain-link cage door. Her teeth on the right side of her mouth were broken. She had a prolapsed vagina, and her mammary glands nearly touched the floor. She didn't even make it to the adoptable-pet runs. The shelter attendant led her directly to the nonpublic kennels for prompt euthanasia. Death row. Who could want such a dog?

Bitsy followed the attendant slowly down the hall, through the maze of runs to her "cell." Walking was difficult for her, but she accepted her fate calmly. No, in reality she did not know her fate and that is perhaps what saved her. As the attendant unhooked the leash from her collar, she looked up at him with utter trust—a dog who had never known any compassion in her own life exuded compassion in what could have been her final hours. She looked at him with the expectation that he would do what was right.

Sodium pentobarbital is the most common method for euthanizing animals in shelters. It's a fast-acting anesthetic that, when given in a lethal dose, overpowers and stops the heart and respiratory system. It's administered with a needle. As the attendant looked down at Bitsy's face, she smiled—the goofy, Labrador "grin" that stretches from ear to ear. Through her own physical frailties, she managed to gather all the goodness of her soul and share it with the attendant who had the most difficult of jobs. It was as if she forgave him. The attendant thought about the syringe filled with sodium pentobarbital, and his shoulders sagged with sadness.

But destiny, if you believe in it, began to play its hand. Through a series of complicated connections involving the shelter attendant and a nearby, reputable breeder who knew Cheryl, Bitsy's fate started to change. Cheryl would come for this dog.

After a week of rain, that December Saturday blazed in sunshine. The winter sun hung low in the sky, yet still gloriously lit our corner of Oregon. It was the type of brisk morning when a simple walk outside makes living worthwhile.

As Cheryl and her husband, Stan, backed out of their driveway, she asked him, "Why are we driving five hours round-trip to rescue a dog? There are plenty who need us right here. And we have no home for her." He merely shook his head and shrugged.

They followed the interstate north, winding through mountains covered with pines and fir trees. Eventually, the curving road settled into the flat and straight stretches of Willamette Valley farmlands.

The Salem shelter is shiny and new. Bricks engraved with donor names pave the entry. Natural light floods the lobby, where several of the most adoptable animals play and romp in special cages and pens. A gift shop sells supplies and toys.

What a difference from our little shelter, Cheryl thought, as she looked around. A young volunteer greeted them warmly and expressed surprise when she learned what dog they had come for. "But that dog is so—," the volunteer said, then stopped herself from saying more. "I'm glad you're here," she added. She directed them to where they needed to go.

Bitsy lay at the kennel door, her raw nose once more pressed against chain link. As Cheryl approached, the dog lifted her head and turned her face to Cheryl. She panted softly. Her brown eyes, the only part of her that did not sag, droop, or bleed, looked directly into Cheryl's eyes, penetrating to her core. It was as if their souls touched.

In a completely logical world, no one would have adopted this dog. But Cheryl recalls she had no control. "When I looked at that physically wrecked dog, I knew she was waiting for me. I felt I had no say. It was already decided that I would take her."

It required both Cheryl and Stan to lift the dog into the back of their car.

"What will we call her?" Stan asked, pausing to catch his breath. "'Bitsy' does not fit."

"Her name is 'Grace,'" Cheryl replied without hesitation. No other name would do. Grace. Yes, it fit. Its many definitions include divine assistance, an act of kindness or clemency, mercy, or pardon.

Grace's final home would not be with Cheryl and Stan who already had a house full of dogs. A few days after returning with Grace, Cheryl got the final call to decide Grace's fate. Lin, another animal lover, telephoned in tears. Her beloved pet boxer had died of cancer.

Lin looks like someone who would have been homecoming queen in high school. She's blonde and blue-eyed. She's animated and has a heart as big as Cheryl's. She directs her strong maternal powers to the benefit of animals now that her own two daughters are grown. With her husband's blessing, she opens their home and two-hundred-acre ranch to stray cats and abandoned dogs. At the time, Lin's family consisted of two basset hounds, a toy poodle, a terrier, an old Lab, and five cats. Lin keeps a vet and an animal groomer quite busy ministering to her flock.

To distract Lin from her grief, Cheryl told her the story of Grace and concluded by asking, "Will you take Grace?"

"Yes," Lin replied.

"Don't you want to meet her first?"

"I don't care what she looks like," Lin said. "She deserves a break."

So, Grace joined Lin's family.

And Cheryl knew her answer for Sheriff Main. "Grace gave me the reason and confidence to say, 'yes.'" she says. "Of all the animals I've helped, Grace stands out. Despite her incredible life of abuse, her spirit remained free and loving. How many other 'Graces' are out there?"

It's been more than a year since Grace joined Lin's family. Lin has overseen the repair of Grace's body. A series of operations have restored much of her physical beauty. Amazingly, her spirit required little healing. Lin describes her as "untarnished." Her smile still shines brightly. She runs freely with the other family dogs on four acres that Lin fenced for them. She has developed a fetish for tennis balls. In the afternoons, she lies on the front porch mat. Flanked by two large flower pots, she looks regal and serene.

At night, she sleeps just outside Lin's bedroom. "She'd sleep *next* to our bed if she didn't snore so loudly," Lin says.

Grace draws people to her. Whenever Lin and her husband entertain, Grace circulates through their friends. Hands reach out to stroke her head or touch her tail as she passes.

When Cheryl visits (which is often), Grace greets her with the love of two kindred souls meeting. As Cheryl tells her story to yet another visitor, Grace leans against Cheryl's leg, closes her eyes peacefully, and listens.

Cheryl has brought together a coalition of animal advocates, including Lin and me, to help privatize the shelter. With support from the county government, we've cleaned up the old cinderblock building, repaired fences, painted, and cleaned. Even the restroom soap dispenser now works. We're developing plans for a new shelter which will quadruple the size; it will have a gift shop and a classroom. We plan to educate the public about proper animal care and preventing abuse. Next month we take over officially as managers.

If you want to adopt an animal, the shelter is easy to find. Just head west off the interstate at exit 129. Pass the log yard and turn right at the drive. Curve up the hill and through the gates. And watch for the new sign out front: "Saving Grace Pet Adoption Center." ❖

❋

July 25

Dear Riley,

I like to eat plants. That really bugs Mom. She always yells, "No, Kilroy!" If I'm really quick, though, I can get a few bites swallowed. Then I walk around in circles while I make really cool belching noises. Eventually, I barf up a little.

We went on a hike today. I didn't want to wander too far, because Mom and her new friend were picking blackberries. Mmmmmm, I love blackberries, but I hate the way the thorns scratch my nose. Sometimes, Mom picks a little one just for me. After lunch, I went off by myself and found a huge patch of blackberries and ate and ate.

Love,

Kilroy

Mmmmmm,
I love blackberries.

※

July 28

Dear Kilroy,

I like to eat funny things, too. I ate a bag of deer repellent once. Mom and Dad knew right away what I had done. Dad picked up the ripped-apart bag, just as Mom was inspecting the yellow powder all over my nose. It's hard to get away with anything.

Mom called the vet to get my stomach pumped. Fortunately, before we left, she found all the pieces of the bag (I tore them up pretty good) and put them back together. She read that the stuff is made out of dried eggs and white pepper, and won't harm pets (that's me). It just made me burp a lot.

Later, I scared away a bunch of deer who were grazing on our lawn. They ran away really fast. Mom said it must've been all that deer repellent inside me.

Love,

Riley

✵

July 31

Dear Riley,

Uh-oh. I ate too many blackberries. It gave me serious diarrhea. Unfortunately, Mom was not at home to let me outside. I tried very hard to wait, but it was impossible. It went everywhere . . . floors, walls . . . yuck. I was so embarrassed.

I sat in the one remaining clean spot on the laundry-room floor and waited until Mom came home. She didn't get mad at all, even though it took two hours late at night to clean everything. She must really love me.

Love,

Kilroy

Tartan was curious,
confident, and full
of enthusiasm.

Animals are such agreeable friends.
They ask no questions, they pass no criticisms.

—GEORGE ELIOT

❦

LESLEY AND TARTAN

The whelping kennels at Guide Dogs' San Rafael, California, campus stay busy year round. About nine hundred pups enter the world there each year. Applications from raisers come in. Puppies go out. What a raiser gets depends on what's available. Yellow Lab. Black Lab. Golden retriever. Lab-golden cross. German shepherd. Male. Female. It's potluck.

But occasionally, it seems like a higher power makes the match. Some pups arrive at just the right moment in a raiser's life, at the moment they are needed most.

Tartan, a male yellow Lab, wasn't even supposed to be Lesley's pup. I met Lesley during the summer when she responded to a meeting notice for new raisers. She, her husband, Len, and daughter, Alysen, faithfully attended our meetings, puppy-sat a couple of our pups, and filled out an application. Straightforward and friendly, Lesley never hesitated to ask questions or express her opinion. I liked her from the beginning.

In the fall, I learned that a black Lab would be delivered to her when the puppy truck stopped in our town in November. I called her to tell her the news. No one was home, so I left a message. A week passed without a call back, so I sent her an e-mail message. This time, Len called back. Lesley was in California, he told me. Her elderly mother had been murdered.

I sat motionless at my desk, the phone receiver clenched in my hand. Silence. I stumbled for something to say. Len said they knew little, but he expected Lesley home in a few days. Finally, I stammered out that I would cancel the puppy delivery. "You don't need to deal with this now," I said. The black Lab went to another raiser in Nevada.

A couple of weeks later, Lesley called. A suspect had been apprehended. He was her mother's handyman. Not much more than that was known, so eventually our conversation came around to the guide pup.

"You know, Nora, I think I still want a pup," Lesley said. I was surprised. "Can you please delay it until after Christmas?" she continued. "I think it would be good for me."

"You have no obligations," I assured her. "But whatever you want, Lesley."

Tartan arrived on a rainy, dreary day in January. Lesley, Len, and Alysen, with tiny Tartan in her arms, posed for my camera under a red umbrella. Lesley is smiling in the photo, but inside I knew she was broken by the violence that had invaded their lives.

The months ahead would bring trip after trip down to California for Lesley. First to clean out her mother's home, then appearances at every court hearing, and eventually the sentencing. Sometimes her family went with her; sometimes they couldn't. But little Tartan made each trip. He lay, curled up on the floor of the passenger side of her car, for the seven-hour trip each way. As Lesley felt the need, she talked to him, and he listened. No questions. No comments. When the unspeakable happens, animals can provide an empathy that humans cannot.

After a day of boxing up her mother's things, Lesley would sit on the floor of her motel room hugging Tartan. His soft warmth enveloped and soothed her. His own needs gave her purpose. No matter what had happened that day, Tartan still needed to be fed, relieved, groomed, and exercised. The public attention a guide pup brings kept Lesley from retreating into herself.

Tartan grew. We joked that he was a size large dog in a size extra-large skin. His fur bunched up in folds around his neck; his ears hung longer than any Lab I'd ever seen; his brown eyes drooped at the corners. He was curious, confident, full of personality and enthusiasm.

Lesley carried a picture of him in her wallet, next to her daughter's photo. "I can't look at that picture without smiling," she said as she showed it to me. "Tartan senses when I need him and comes to me. Even our pet dog doesn't do that. Do you think it's possible that he can read my mind?"

"I don't know," I said. But actually I think the bond between them was so strong that Tartan could anticipate Lesley's needs by the slightest change in her body language. Perhaps that is mind reading.

Tartan was with Lesley when she learned more details of the crime. Her mother had interrupted the handyman burglarizing her house. Visualizing the last moments of her mother's life was more than Lesley could stand. She started seeing a counselor. Tartan accompanied her. I bumped into her in the medical building lobby. Tartan, in his green guide-pup jacket, sat calmly by her side, watching her every move. As we chatted, he maneuvered himself so he sat on Lesley's feet.

"He hates bare floors," Lesley explained.

At home, she gave Tartan a down-filled pillow to sleep on next to her bed. He loved it and would often put himself to bed if the family stayed up too late.

Her mother's death had left Lesley feeling vulnerable and fearful. Her counselor put a name to it: post-traumatic stress disorder, the same condition that a war veteran can experience. "Tartan is a complete wimp," she said with a slight smile, "but I feel safer with him."

Lesley worked hard with Tartan. His high energy sometimes created training challenges. We talked frequently about different techniques to use with him. She wanted him to have every chance for success as a guide dog, to become the eyes for someone who needed him. The effort he required pulled Lesley outside of herself and allowed her to focus on the needs of someone else. She was healing.

The one-year anniversary of her mother's death passed. In December, Lesley and I sat across from each other on a double-decker bus tour of Christmas lights. Other raisers and guide pups filled the top deck. We rubbed away the window fog to peer at the sparkling lights spelling out "peace, hope, love."

"For the first time in a long time, I feel lighter, not so depressed," Lesley confided to me quietly. Tartan lay in the aisle between us. "I don't think I could have survived this past year without my family—and Tartan." At the mention of his name, Tartan gazed up adoringly at her.

Others might say that any dog would have helped Lesley, but Lesley would disagree: "Tartan is special. He was the perfect dog for me." And that's all that matters. If Lesley believes it, then it is true. Somehow, Tartan, the perfect dog for Lesley, was matched with Lesley when she needed him most.

The man who took her mother's life was sentenced to twenty-five years to life in a California prison. "I don't think about him anymore," she said. A few weeks later, the puppy truck came to take Tartan away to start his formal training.

"I can't believe he's leaving me," Lesley said as the truck drove away. But I think she knew that his job with her was done. "His life will have two purposes," she added thoughtfully. "He has helped me. Now it is time for him to do the job he was born to do."

Six months later, on the last day of June, Tartan graduated as a guide dog. We met Rob, his new fifty-two-year-old blind partner, before the graduation ceremony on Guide Dogs' Oregon campus.

"I asked the trainers for a strong and confident guide," Rob told us as we sat together in the dormitory library. He was getting all of that in Tartan. Rob works as an urban planner for the city of Seattle. He travels with his work and faces the noise and confusion of downtown Seattle daily. Tartan will keep him safe.

Tartan looked great. He had finally grown into his size extra-large skin. He was muscular and broad in the shoulders. He had matured into a very handsome dog. Lesley wrapped her arms around his neck and hugged him hard, but then gently placed his leash back in Rob's hands. Tartan nuzzled her fingers, then he looked back at Rob and shifted his weight so that he leaned against Rob's knee.

After the ceremony, Rob and Tartan left for Seattle to start their new life together. Lesley and her family had one more stop to make.

In the hills above Portland, the Willamette National Cemetery covers 270 acres with gently rolling slopes of neatly trimmed grass and row after row of granite markers, flush with the lawn. Lesley knew right where to go. As I got out of the car, she was already heading across the grass. She slipped out of her high-heeled sandals and strode barefoot about three hundred feet to where the manicured lawn disappeared into the thick growth of evergreens that edged the entire cemetery. Lesley's husband, Len, and daughter, Alysen, followed closely behind.

There at the edge of the cemetery, where a large cedar tree stands tall, at the bottom of a slight rise, her mother is buried. I stayed back while they stood by the headstone, arms entwined around each other.

It was nearly six o'clock, but the summer sun still shone strong and warm. The cobalt-blue sky with just a few clouds arched over us. The silence was broken only by the song of a distant meadowlark. As the three of them returned to the car, I walked over to the marker. Four wild daisies, picked from the undergrowth beneath the cedar tree, lay across the engraved granite. One from Len, one from Alysen, one from Lesley, and one from Tartan. ❖

※

August 2

Dear Kilroy,

I went fishing today. No, really . . . *I* went fishing. Mom and I hiked down to the river. A little girl was fishing (with some help from her dad). He said no fish were biting. Just then, the little bobber ball on her line started going up and down. "Fish on! Fish on!" yelled the dad. "Reel it in!"

The little girl started turning her reel, but the knot to her bobber thingie came undone. The line came in empty. She started to cry. The bobber still was going up and down. Mom said, "Riley . . . get the ball!" I jumped in the river and swam to the bobber. I grabbed it in my mouth and brought it back onto the shore—with the fish still attached! Everybody told me I was a good boy. I was very proud.

Love,

Riley

※

August 5

Dear Riley,

Wow, what a fishing story! Will you teach me how to fish? No, wait a minute. You better teach me how to swim first. How about this weekend?

Love,

Kilroy

✺

August 10

Dear Riley,

Thanks for the swimming lesson last weekend. I'll try to remember: paddle hard, head up, paddle hard, head up. I just hate it when water gets in my nose and eyes. Mom got me some cool goggles, but this swimming stuff is still hard.

Love,

Kilroy

*Mom got me
some cool goggles.*

Saffron sank.

※

August 16

Dear Kilroy,

Take it one step at a time. Saffron can't swim very well either. We were all down at the river, along the edge. Saffron stepped off a rock and *sank*. Mom was very surprised and pulled her out. Saffron thought it was fun and wanted to do it again.

Love,

Riley

*Whenever Saffron donned her
green jacket, she became
serious and exuded confidence.*

The best and most beautiful things in the world
cannot be seen or even touched.
They must be felt with the heart.
—HELEN KELLER

❧

SAFFRON AND THE
WOMAN ON THE TRAIN

Saffron left us today. The large, white Guide Dogs for the Blind truck drove away with her in it. She is gone. Her blue rug next to my desk is empty, save for the platinum blonde hairs she left behind. A half-devoured chew bone lies nearby.

Saffron is a yellow Labrador retriever. She was born at the Guide Dogs whelping kennel and spent her first year here in our community, learning good house manners and being socialized in public settings. My friend Kelly and I shared the responsibility of raising her. Now she will live under the gentle direction of professional trainers. They will teach her to guide a visually impaired person.

Last month, Saffron and I rode the train to Seattle. I wanted one more urban adventure with her before she left. There was so much I still wanted to show her, teach her. But Saffron would show me that weekend that she was a capable teacher, too.

Saffron quickly boarded the train, her green Guide Dog in Training jacket attracting the attention of her fellow travelers. It never failed: Whenever Saffron donned her green jacket, she stood more erect; she became serious and exuded confidence, as if she knew it meant something very important.

One fortyish woman a couple rows ahead sought us out. Her softly curled, chestnut hair set off a wide smile. She joined us in the dining car and asked about the guide-dog program. As the miles whizzed by, the woman opened up. I don't know if it was the anonymity of train travel or the presence of Saffron, but the woman spoke of things not normally shared by strangers.

Her life had been hard but fascinating. She had escaped from Hungary as a teenager, leaving behind an infant son. Recently, she had begun to doubt her chosen profession of hospital ministry. She admitted to spiraling down into deep depression. I listened for an hour. What help could I offer this woman? What advice? All I could do was nod and murmur assurances.

Saffron lay quietly, her head resting on the woman's foot. I watched as the woman absentmindedly stroked Saffron's white-gold head. A sense of peace passed between them.

Then, it occurred to me: I didn't have to say anything. Saffron was giving her everything she needed. Warmth, attention, affection, an open heart.

As we neared her departure point, the woman knelt down and petted Saffron from head to tail. Saffron stood and leaned hard against the woman's leg—a "canine hug."

The woman looked back up at me with eyes shiny. "Thank you," she whispered, her voice catching slightly. "Thank you for sharing your dog."

I will never see this woman again, and I've already forgotten her name. But I haven't forgotten the magical tranquility of the hour we three spent together.

I remember that trip now as I look at Saffron's empty, blue rug. Saffron may not make it as a working guide dog. Only about a third of the pups graduate as guides. But she's already touched the lives of those around her, and she reminded me that sometimes words are not necessary. Sometimes listening is all that is required. Sometimes all that's needed is a hug. ❖

✺

August 25

Dear Kilroy,

My sister Saffron is doing great. Mom gets weekly report cards from the school about her progress. She's in training phase six (of nine). She's learning how to get on escalators now and be responsible for her partner's safety. She has to learn to identify potential dangers and decide what to do. Do you remember learning all that stuff when you were in training? You know, it's kind of like having a sister away at med school. I'm very proud of her. But if she decides not to be a "doctor" and chooses another career, that's okay with me. Just like you—you changed careers. Your job as "Chief Knucklehead" for your family is very important.

This weekend, Mom and Dad will be in Los Angeles. I get to go to my sitter's house. They have a little golden retriever named Lacey. I can usually sneak up onto the bed with one of my sitter's three little girls.

One night when I slept on the floor, the youngest daughter cuddled up with me and slept all night on the floor, too. I love staying at my sitter's house.

Love from your cousin,

Riley

※☼※

August 28

Dear Riley,

Thanks for the news about Saffron. It brought back some good memories. Sometimes, I miss the trainers at school. They were all very nice.

You're sure lucky to be able to spend the night at someone's house. Once in a while I get to stay with Poppie (Mom's dad). It's nice, but he never sleeps on the floor with me.

Love from your knucklehead cousin,

Kilroy

*Riley seemed to
sense he needed
to look after her.*

A mother understands what a child does not say.

—JEWISH PROVERB

❀

ELEANOR

When my sisters, brother, and I first started to suspect that our mother had Alzheimer's disease, public knowledge of the illness was not high. This was before made-for-TV movies dramatized its devastating effects, before talk-show hosts interviewed the afflicted, before former President Reagan made his heart-wrenching announcement that he suffered from the disease.

We began noticing changes in Mom sometime after my wedding. I know this because the photo taken of us that day is the last I have of her where she looks like the Mom of my memories. We stand, arms around each other, smiling broadly, and looking directly into the camera. In later photos, her unfocused eyes and uncomfortable stance reveal the confusion within.

At first, the changes were minor, mainly forgetfulness. Our mother's doctor passed off her symptoms as "hardening of the arteries." But our own sleuthing said otherwise. The increasing signs were impossible to ignore. She repeated the same question five, ten times a day. She mixed up or completely forgot words. She constantly lost things—her glasses, her flashlight. A few years later, she lost herself. At a family reunion, a cousin found her wandering the campground; she'd gotten lost in the fifty feet between the campsite and the restroom.

A series of mental and physical tests with a neurologist confirmed our suspicions. Dad did his best to care for her. They had met when Mom skipped third grade and joined his class.

"Eleanor was the smart, little red-haired girl in the front row," Dad always said. They married after World War II and quickly added four children to the baby-boom generation: Alice, Frank, Kathie, and Nora. I was the last and was named for her; my given name "Nora Lee" contains all the letters of "Eleanor," just rearranged. Mom and Dad celebrated their forty-fourth wedding anniversary the week that Mom was finally diagnosed.

"I promised her 'in sickness and in health,'" Dad told us. "I will take care of her."

All of us helped, but Dad, as primary caregiver, took on the most. Nine years had passed since we first noticed the symptoms of her illness, nearly a decade of watching her slowly lose the skills for everyday living. Her dependence on Dad grew. He bathed and dressed her. He cooked and cleaned and shopped—and grew tired.

Even with his best intentions, we knew he would reach his limits. Alice and I researched care facilities. "Just in case," we told Dad. We settled on a homey facility that offered progressive care. The more-functional residents lived in the bedroom suites of a sprawling, turn-of-the-century home. Later, if their needs changed, they could move to the new wing that offered a higher level of care.

Less than a month later, I got a desperate call from Dad. Mom had failed to recognize him. She had run from their house screaming. The police came. Paramedics arrived. Mom was found, and she finally remembered who Dad was. But the incident devastated Dad and the rest of us. Our shy, gentle mother was losing her mind. We arranged for Mom to move to the facility.

On my first visit, Mom met me with tears. "Your father has divorced me," she confided.

I did my best to reassure her. "No, no. Dad will be by later," I said. "And Kathie is coming from Seattle tomorrow. Next week, Frank will be here, too."

But in her state, she only knew confusion and depression. I led her out to the sun-drenched porch. We found some chairs, and I held her hand, as the sun warmed us. Webster, the resident tuxedo-colored cat, strolled over to us and rubbed against my leg. I picked him up and placed him in Mom's lap. She stroked his neck, and he began to purr loudly. "Nice puppy," she cooed. I did not correct her.

Over the next few months, we regularly sat on the porch in the sun. When words and memories failed her, Webster distracted and calmed her.

On Mother's Day, I brought Mom to our house and sat her in a chair on the lawn as I planted pansies, her favorite flowers. Riley sat beside her. He seemed to sense he needed to look after her. He rested his black head on her knee. Mom smoothed his ears.

"What a handsome . . . handsome . . ." Her voice faltered.

"Dog." I finished for her.

I asked the director of Mom's care facility for permission to bring Riley. As the spring days warmed and lengthened into summer, we sought out the shade instead of the sun. I moved our chairs under the stately oaks surrounding the old home. Across the road, fields of wild mustard bloomed yellow.

Some days we said nothing; some days she told me the stories of her youth. That's the way the disease is. The most recent memories fade first; the oldest stay around the longest. I'd heard all the stories so many times, but for her, each time was the first.

She'd close her eyes and be back living on her grandparents' Wisconsin dairy farm during the Depression. She'd talk about picking wild strawberries in the summer with her friend Frances. She'd remember walking to school in weather so cold that she got frostbite. ("See, see this red spot on my nose? That's where the frostbite was.") She'd smile with pride when she described how her poem won the student writing contest.

If she struggled for a word, I'd help. Here was a woman who had lived her life in love with words, but now the simplest ones tripped her. When I was growing up, together we often consulted our huge, two-volume dictionary. Words, reading, writing, education—Mom valued them highly and instilled these same values in her children. She worked for the mentally gifted student program in our school district before she retired. When I was in high school, Mom and I often took evening walks to discuss the day, my schoolwork, or anything troubling me.

During a visit at summer's end, she looked at me with no recognition. We were sitting in the old home's living room, near the fireplace. Riley lay asleep at our feet. I took my cue from her, not wanting to upset her. For the next hour, I chatted with her like a friend.

As I prepared to go, she patted Riley's head. "Bye bye, Buddy," she said, calling him by the name of her favorite dog from childhood. Then she turned to me. "You remind me so much of my youngest daughter, Nora. I hope you can meet her sometime."

I concentrated hard on holding my smile and keeping the mood light. "I'd like that," I replied and turned to go. Outside, I sank down onto the porch steps. I buried my head in Riley's neck, leaving a wet streak on his fur.

Eventually, Mom moved to the secure, higher-level-of-care wing. During her last nine months, she lived in a nursing home. Mercifully, she died of other medical problems before the Alzheimer's completely robbed her of herself. Ten days before Christmas, she slipped into a coma. I remember thinking how inappropriate the carolers sounded as they sang "Joy to the World" in the hallway outside her room. She passed away, as I held her hand.

When spring came again, I stopped by the old home with the stately oaks and the sun-drenched porch. I brought Riley with me. I greeted and thanked the staff for their good care of our mother. As I passed through the living room, an old man sat by himself near the fireplace. His face betrayed the vacant look of the disease that had stolen my mother. I took Riley over to him.

Riley sat next to him, then rested his head on the man's knee. Instinctively, the man began to pet Riley. A slight smile curled up the corners of his mouth.

"What a nice . . . nice . . . " His voice drifted off.

"Dog." I finished for him. ❖

※

September 22

Dear Kilroy,

Here's an important job for every good pet: At suppertime, make sure your mom promptly quits whatever she is doing and feeds you. If she is working at the computer, use your nose to throw her arm off the keyboard. If she is reading a book, put your head in her lap and look up at her. Make sure the whites of your eyes show at the bottom. They always think this is very cute. When all else fails, pick up your supper dish in your mouth and bring it to her. If dinnertime is 5 P.M., start acting like this around 4 P.M. or sooner. If you're very good at it, you may be able to get dinner moved up earlier and earlier every day.
Love,
Riley

✺

September 27

Dear Riley,

We've moved to a new house. It's bigger than our last place. It has a wonderful, large backyard. Mom says there's a cute little bunny that lives under our garden shed. I haven't seen him yet, but I sure can tell where he's been hopping.

I love to dash around with my nose to the ground following his scent. Sometimes I come across some of his droppings. Boy, are they tasty. Mom gets grossed out, when she sees me eating them, so I try to be sneaky about it.

Love,

Kilroy

✺

September 29

Dear Kilroy,

Yum. We've got wild turkeys around our house. They leave me little treats. You'll have to try them next time you visit.

Love,

Riley

※

October 23

Dear Riley,

Have you ever met a kitten in person? I just met one, and she sure isn't very friendly.

Tessa brought her home to live with us. I wanted to make sure that little kitten felt welcome, so I ran right up to say hello. Guess what she did? She spit in my face and smacked my nose with her tiny, little paw. She really scared me. I ran down the hall and peeked at her from around the corner of the bedroom door.

I don't know what to do.

Love,

Kilroy

*Cats get
better with age.*

※

October 28

Dear Kilroy,

Cats get better with age. At our house we have an old black one named Bart. He sleeps all day in the sun by the door. We pretty much ignore each other, but every now and then we chase each other for fun. Once, on a very cold day, we curled up together. It wasn't too bad. Give your kitten time and space. Don't startle her. Oh, and one more thing . . . as tempting as cat food is, DON'T eat it. It has the same effect as blackberries.

Speaking of cats, yesterday, Mom, Dad, and I were coming home from fishing. We hiked up the river bank, across the bluff, and headed toward home. I smelled something wonderful, and away I went. Wouldn't you know, it was only a cat. Black like Bart, but with a white stripe down its back and tail. You know, it didn't smell like Bart, though. As I got closer to check it out, Mom and Dad caught up with me. They both saw the cat at the same time and yelled, "RILEY, NO!" Just then, the cat lifted its tail, and *gadzooks*, what a smell.

Mom and Dad had already taken off running. Dad's fishing net was banging against his leg. Mom's pack was swaying on her back. I sprinted right by them and didn't look back. I was sure that cat was chasing all three of us.

Finally, I stopped in a clearing. Mom and Dad came huffin' and puffin' up behind me. The cat was nowhere. We had escaped!

It would've been a perfect day, except Mom gave me a bath when we got home.

Love,

Riley

They touched noses.

> *Do you think dogs will be in heaven?*
> *I tell you, they will be there long before any of us.*
> —Robert Louis Stevenson

❈

JASPER

Technically, Nash was the first guide-dog puppy in our club. He was a "baby pup," eight weeks old when he arrived. But really, another dog was our first. Yellow Lab Jasper came to us as a "teenager," a six-month-old dog, from another club a couple weeks before Nash arrived. It's not that I've forgotten Jasper. No, it is because remembering him is painful. Jasper's story isn't a happy one. In fact, it's the kind of story most of us don't like to tell. But I must tell it if we are to remember him. Jasper was a dog that never got the chance to realize his potential.

Jasper was a platinum-blonde Lab, like Saffron, but even lighter. His almost-white fur made his dark-brown eyes and wide, happy smile stand out even more. He was expressive and joyful. Pat, our Guide Dogs adviser, personally delivered him to us at one of our meetings. Rebecca, his quiet, thirteen-year-old raiser, took his leash from Pat, and promptly fell in love with him. She adored animals; she had a menagerie at home. She lived in the country on acreage surrounded by the vineyards of a nearby winery. They had plenty of room for their assortment of animals. But Jasper would be special. As we do with all guide pups, she would take him everywhere. He would be with her constantly. Sleep in her bedroom. Go to school with her. Accompany her shopping. Such 'round-the-clock companionship builds a bond quickly.

Rebecca had been my first recruit. She responded to an article in the newspaper about the formation of our club. She and I attended our first all-day orientation together. We ate lunch at a nearby MacDonald's during our noon break. Her grandmother was blind, she told me as we munched our hamburgers. Rebecca had personally witnessed the hardships and challenges of the visually impaired. Here was her way to help.

Rebecca was a natural dog handler. She was firm, demonstrative, and affectionate. She was a bit lanky, not much muscle on her thin arms. Jasper weighed about sixty pounds—a lot of dog to handle, but her timing was excellent. The moment Jasper moved out of line, she immediately corrected him, then praised him when he responded.

When Rebecca could not make one of our meetings, I took Jasper for the day. Together, we made my round of errands. With his green jacket on, we cruised the aisles of the grocery store. He followed my cart sedately. As I contemplated the Shredded Wheat and Cheerios, he sat patiently and visually inspected the kiddie cereals on the bottom shelf.

About halfway down the aisle, a small boy, not much taller than Jasper, exclaimed to his mother, "There's a *dog* in here!"

Apparently his mom knew a little about service dogs. She took his hand to keep him from bolting down the aisle to play with Jasper. "He's a working dog, honey," she patiently explained. "We need to let him do his job."

I smiled at them, as our carts passed. Jasper snuck a quick lick of the little boy's face, which was even with his own. The boy giggled in delight and wiped the wet kiss from his cheek.

Later, with the groceries put away in the car, I decided to take Jasper to the duck pond next to the store. We found an empty bench. A cool, spring breeze floated off the pond. Jasper's ears and nose went into full alert as a flock of geese waddled and honked at water's edge, not more than twenty feet away. His muscles tensed, but he did not move.

In the water, a nutria paddled by. Nutrias, otter-like mammals, are common around here. I watched it absentmindedly before I realized this one was different. It was white, as white as Jasper. It swam into a rock, bumping against it. Apparently, like many albino animals, its eyesight was poor. It maneuvered around the rock and headed toward us, waddling up the bank. I backed away, but it kept coming. I realized it could not see me. It picked up Jasper's scent and turned to him. Before I could react, they touched noses. Startled, the nutria spun around and fled back to the water. Jasper watched it retreat, as amazed as I was by the encounter. He made no attempt to pursue it. I praised him for his calm and confident behavior.

"Oh Jasper, you'll be a terrific guide dog," I said as I stroked his back. He looked back at me affectionately; a little bit of white showed beneath his brown eyes. He seemed to know he was a very good dog.

At the meeting that evening, Pat was quite pleased with his progress. I considered keeping him overnight, but I knew Rebecca missed him. It was nearly 10 P.M. by the time I delivered him back to her house.

About twenty-four hours later, she called. "Jasper is throwing up," she said. He had taken some water, but he was not able to keep food down. Throwing up is not that uncommon in dogs. I was concerned, but not overly so.

"Take him to the vet in the morning if he's not better," I advised.

He wasn't, so she did. An xray revealed an obstruction in Jasper's intestine. Labs are notorious for ingesting almost anything. They pick things up in their mouths, and sometimes they swallow them. It can happen in a flash, the one moment you're not paying attention. Jasper required emergency surgery.

Dr. Ross performed the operation. He found a length of tough carpet string in Jasper. It was probably the worst thing he could have eaten. It had acted as a saw on his intestines, allowing toxic fecal matter to escape into his abdomen. Dr. Ross completed the repair. Jasper was now in the vet hospital's intensive care unit, doped up on pain killers and antibiotics. They planned to keep him several days.

He made it, I thought with relief. I prayed that he would recover fully with no aftereffects that would prevent him from becoming a guide.

Twelve hours later, Dr. Ross called. Jasper had made it through the night, but then had gone into shock and died. "It happened very quickly," he said. The damage had been extensive. There just were not enough antibiotics to overcome the poison within him.

How could this happen? I thought. The first dog entrusted to my care, my supervision, was dead. A good dog. A very good dog. And now I had to call Rebecca and tell her.

Rebecca buried Jasper behind her house. The surrounding grapevines were starting to show signs of new growth. She marked the spot with some large, heavy stones.

At our next meeting, Rebecca and her mother walked quietly up to me and handed me all of Jasper's training supplies.

"Please stay," I said. But she shook her head silently. I think she was afraid if she tried to speak, she would cry. They turned and left.

Her grief mirrored mine. I wanted to follow her out. I felt like quitting, too. I felt responsible. Did Jasper ingest that string when he was with me? Or, if not, maybe if I had kept him overnight he would not have eaten it at Rebecca's house. Or what if I had told her to take him immediately to the vet? What if, what if. It didn't matter now. He was dead.

Pat assured me that it was not my fault. "You did all you could," she said. "Sometimes, these things happen." In the end, I decided to stay with the program. Rebecca did not.

Five years later I saw her again. I was giving an orientation to some high school leadership students who wanted to volunteer at our county animal shelter. The tall, lanky girl at the back of the group looked familiar. Finally, at the end of the session, I approached her.

"I'm Rebecca," she said simply. "Jasper's raiser."

Of course. She was a young woman now, but she still had the quiet, competent manner I remembered. She told me she was headed to California in the fall, to college. She planned to major in science.

Rebecca spent all day at the animal shelter taking the penned-up dogs out for fresh air and exercise. She particularly liked a big brown dog. At the end of the day, she took him home on approval. She said her next-door neighbor was looking for a dog like him. She thought they would be a good match.

When I got home, Riley and I walked down to the river. Spring had come, and the surrounding hills were showing signs of new life. Some geese honked as they flew by overhead. The river was clear and cold. As much as Riley loves to swim, he stayed by my side. I thought about Rebecca and Jasper. I was relieved that Rebecca's love of animals was still part of who she was.

And Jasper. He was too young when he died. He never got the chance to become the calm, confident guide I knew he could have been.

I could say something like "I am a better person because of him." But, even though it's true, it sounds too self-serving. Honestly, when I think about Jasper, I still feel a hollow sadness. I wish I could change what happened. But some things we cannot change, no matter how much we wish. It happened, and I've come to accept that. ❖

✻

October 25

Dear Kilroy,

I don't feel very good. I didn't even finish my breakfast this morning. Mom is worried. She felt all over my body, lifted each leg, looked in my mouth. I whimpered when she hugged me gently. I can't sleep. I stay very still, looking at the wall. Well, I did fall asleep for a little bit. When I woke up, I moved a little and cried. Have you ever felt this way? What did your mom do to make you better?
Love,
Riley

❋

October 27

Dear Riley,

I'm sad that you aren't feeling well. I've never been sick, unless you count the blackberries. Oh, and once when I had a limp. When that happened, it was really hard to have Mom look right into my eyes with such concern, and say, "Kilroy, you knucklehead, what's wrong? Where does it hurt?"

At that moment, I certainly wished I could talk. She just sat on the floor with me and held my head in her lap. I always love that. I'm very worried about you, Riley. Write to me soon so I know how you are doing.

Love and licks,

Kilroy

❂

October 29

Dear Kilroy,

I finally was able to tell Mom what was wrong. She had me in her office and watched me all day. Whenever I tried to lie down, my neck hurt, and I cried.

Mom said maybe I pinched a nerve. Just by chance, a friend who is a vet stopped by. He looked me over and agreed with Mom about the pinched nerve. I'm taking some pills which help stop the hurt. I'm supposed to be better in a couple days.

Love,

Riley

❋

October 31

Dear Carol,

I hear you're interested in becoming a puppy-raising leader. Terrific! Don't worry—experience is not required. My only dog-training background was attending obedience classes with my pet Lab about ten years ago.

I originally wanted to raise one guide pup, but there was no club in my area, so I became a club leader by default.

I love dogs and had admired the guide-dog program since I was a kid. I am very impressed with the amount of support that the organization gives its raisers: newsletters, training sessions, equipment, vet care, and so on.

People-handling skills are as important as dog-handling skills (actually, more so). As a leader you are a cheerleader, a nag, a recruiter, an organizer, a communicator, a paper pusher (just a little), a counselor, and a friend to your raisers. Occasionally, you are a dog trainer. If you adore dogs, but don't really like people, you should *not* be a leader.

Not all your pups will become guides. But I have found success and satisfaction in other unexpected ways:

- The single woman who receives a career-change dog and finds great love and companionship.

- The painfully shy girl who bursts with pride when she visits an elementary school with her pup to talk about the program.
- The family who recently lost a loved one and finds comfort in their pup.

And, of course, when a pup does become a guide, there is enormous pride among the whole club. We have changed someone's life beyond belief. If you have any questions, please don't hesitate to call me.

All the best,
Nora

❋

November 1

Dear Nora,

Congratulations! It is our pleasure to notify you that Saffron is graduating as a Guide Dog. We invite you and your family to attend the graduation ceremony and to officially present Saffron to her new blind partner.

Please see the attached schedule for graduation day, so that you may plan your trip.

The graduation ceremony is a wonderful experience for all participants, and it is one more way for us to say thank you for the critical role you play in our mission of service to the blind. We deeply appreciate the combined efforts of you, your family, your leader, and your community in raising Saffron.

Sincerely,
Puppy Raising and Dog Placement Department
Guide Dogs for the Blind

Saffron settled down
and lay quietly
at Colleen's feet.

The first time I walked with my new guide dog,
I felt like I was flying.
She gives me confidence, freedom, and dignity.

—VICKI JACK

❧

GRADUATION

Saffron is a guide dog. She graduated last month at the Guide Dogs for the Blind training campus. She now lives about 150 miles away with Colleen, her thirty-eight-year-old blind partner.

As one of her raisers, I was invited to the graduation ceremony that followed four weeks of intensive on-campus and city work with Colleen. Saffron had already completed five months of formal training with professional handlers.

Jon and I arrived about an hour before the ceremony to allow some time for me to meet and visit with Colleen, and see Saffron once again. I waited in the dormitory library, as an instructor went to Colleen's room. I trembled slightly in anticipation.

Saffron was nearly two years old now, and her entire life had been directed to this moment. I had missed her more than I thought I would over the past six months. We all know from the beginning that these dogs are only on loan to us, but that doesn't stop us from giving them our hearts.

At the end of the hall, a door opened, and two figures and a dog emerged. Saffron! I knew her immediately, even though the green Guide Dog in Training jacket was gone. In its place, the guide-dog harness. I could feel my throat constricting. I swallowed hard.

As they entered the library, Saffron began wiggling and wagging. She remembered me. I tried to ignore her and greet Colleen first, but I couldn't help it. I reached down to the white-gold furry head, then stopped, remembering my guide-dog manners.

"Is it okay if I pet her?" I asked Colleen. She nodded. I stroked and rubbed Saffron's face. We went through the same wiggle greeting when Kelly, my friend and Saffron's co-raiser, arrived. Finally, she settled down and lay quietly at Colleen's feet.

Colleen volunteers four days a week at a senior day-care center. Saffron will guide her via sidewalks and bus travel to and from the center. The trainers did a special session there to make sure Saffron wouldn't react to wheelchairs or walkers. I chuckled, because I knew Saffron would be fine. Every year we hold two or three meetings at nursing/retirement homes. The pups ride the elevators and visit residents. It's excellent socialization for the pups. And long ago with my own mom, I learned how much an animal's visit can mean to someone in a care facility.

Ten minutes before the ceremony, Colleen was led away to the auditorium stage. All the raisers and dogs were brought to a small room off stage. About fifteen people and twelve dogs filled the little room. Golden retrievers, Labradors, a German shepherd. They were all calmly lying or sitting, nose to butt. One massive yellow Lab rested his head on the back of a Lab-golden cross.

I sat on the floor with Saf's head in my lap. I slowly stroked her velvet ears, and she fell asleep.

Images of our year together passed through my mind. Our train trip to Seattle. Swimming at the river. Saffron napping on her blue rug while I worked. I knew that these minutes would be the last in which I could claim her as "mine."

One by one, the raisers went up onto the stage with their dog and passed the leash to the blind partner.

Colleen had quite a fan club at the ceremony. When she stood to receive Saffron, her family and friends jumped up and belted out the old Donovan song:

"I'm just mad about Saffron.
Saffron's mad about me.
They call me mellow yellow . . . ."

Everyone in the packed auditorium, about three hundred people, laughed and clapped.

Then it was our turn.

Saffron, Kelly, and I climbed the three short steps to the stage. The leash passed out of my hands into Colleen's. In her brief speech, Colleen called Saffron "my angel."

I've heard it said that within every guide dog beats the heart of a puppy raiser. That's how I feel now. A little part of my heart is missing. But I only need to remember how Saffron stood protectively by Colleen's side to know that all is as it should be. ❖

※

November 11

Dear Riley,

I am master of the giant slobber. If I don't lick my chops well enough after I take a drink of water, I can make a big ol' drool hang from my lips and nearly touch the ground. It's way cool. Mom thinks it's gross.

Today, purely by accident, I added my own special touch to the drool phenomenon. It was brilliant. I was standing outside by the sliding door looking at my reflection in the glass and admiring the ten-inch drool suspended from my jowls. When I turned my head quickly to check out a low-flying bird, the drool swung around and stuck to the glass. I turned back, amazed.

There I stood, a handsome yellow Lab, delicately connected to the door by a glistening strand of dog slobber. Truly majestic! Mom was inside—heading for the Windex.

Love,

Kilroy

Our pups entertained themselves.

A dog teaches you fidelity, perseverance,
and to turn around three times before lying down.

—ROBERT BENCHLEY

❋

THE PARADE

Jon does not share my passion for dogs. He likes them, and he loves Riley. But, frankly, at times, he's a little irritated by the disruption caused by the parade of dogs through our home.

I take care of friends' dogs when they go on vacation. I evaluate guide pups. I foster dogs from the shelter. Jon tolerates the invasion because he loves me and knows it's important to me. Many of these dogs are young pups who may not have learned all their manners yet. We've had a lamp tipped over by an exuberant golden retriever; sleep disrupted by a homesick-howling Labrador; a favorite slipper chewed up; a wicker basket destroyed; an occasional puppy-relieving accident; and on and on.

Jon's approach to life can be quite different from mine, but those differences have kept our marriage interesting and stimulating for more than twenty years.

I am the right-brain thinker in the family—the creative one with a liberal arts education, willing to take things as they come.

He is an aerospace engineer with a scientific background. He thinks logically and likes things in their proper order.

There is nothing logical or orderly about an eight-week-old yellow Labrador who is spending her first night away from her littermates. She will probably cry and whine to a level that is very difficult for the human ear to tolerate—especially at 4 A.M.

So when Jon expressed interest in joining our guide-dog group in our community parade, I was delighted. The Saturday-morning, Main Street parade is an annual event that celebrates Father's Day weekend. For a small town, it's a big deal. The downtown merchants hold a sidewalk sale. Neighbors greet neighbors, as they line the parade route. Little children perch on their dads' shoulders for the best view.

The first year we participated, Jon stayed home. I was disappointed, but went ahead with the plans. We wore white shirts and blue jeans; we brushed our dogs; we washed their green jackets and trimmed their toenails. We practiced walking in step and staying in rows. We placed the guide pups and their raisers in the front; career-change dogs fell in step behind. I led our pack with Saffron, my guide pup. Lesley and Tartan walked beside me. In the back row, Alice with Kilroy marched next to Sherry with Nash.

We were entry number 36. Number 35 was the Parade Queen and her court. Mounted on flower-draped horses, the young women looked radiant. They wore cowboy hats with tiaras sparkling across the front. Unfortunately, they did not provide their own pooper-scooper crew. Our neatly formed rows fell apart as we maneuvered among the horse piles. We did not win a prize.

At dinner, I regaled Jon with tales of well-behaved dogs and obedience drills. He half-listened. When I mentioned the antique cars that followed us, he perked up.

"What kind? Who was driving? Were they restored?" he asked.

Ah-hah. I had his interest.

"Maybe next year I can come," he added.

"Sure." I replied enthusiastically.

But I quickly learned Jon didn't plan to walk with a dog. No, he wanted to lead our group by riding one of his vintage motor scooters. Jon's collection of scooters includes a 1952 Cushman Eagle, a matching set of '59 Mustangs (not the cars—these Mustangs are small, high-powered motorcycles), a 1968 Lambretta, and a 1962 Cushman Trailmaster. Jon is a perfectionist, and the collection reflects that.

The following June he rolled out his Cushman Eagle. He washed and waxed it. He gassed it up and polished the chrome. I made a "Guide Dog Puppies" sign for the back. He trailered it down to the courthouse parking lot and unloaded it there among the horse trailers and popcorn wagons.

The day held promise of being a hot one, so we waited beneath the one-hundred-year-old elm tree that spreads gracefully over half of the courthouse lawn. Our pups entertained themselves or lounged in the semi-damp grass as the cacophony of parade preparations went on around us. Across the street, the bagpipe marching men in their kilts warmed up with squawks and squeals. Three teenaged girls tended to a herd (is that what it's called?) of alpacas that sported red streamers. A log truck bedecked with American flags rumbled by.

As we waited, Jon checked his oil level. Alice and Kilroy mingled with the career-change dogs. Since career-change dogs can no longer wear the coveted green jacket, we tied green bandannas around their necks—a way to signify they will always be special and a part of our group.

Alice brought a friend she wanted me to meet; he wandered over to talk to Jon, who was now wiping down the Cushman again, polishing a water spot that only he could see.

I checked us in and was pleased to learn that we would follow the Sweet Sensations preteen dance drill team. No horses were ahead of us this year. What a relief.

I pinned our entry number (14) on Jon's shirt. For good measure,

I tied a green career-change bandanna around his neck. He looked great—a '50s dude riding his '50s scooter.

Meanwhile, the Sweet Sensations (entry number 13), in their blue-sequined and white-fringed outfits, practiced. Their theme music blared out of a loudspeaker mounted on the back of flatbed truck. By the third complete run-through, the heavy-beat music rattled nonstop in my head.

This year, we felt like parade pros. Now we had club shirts—yellow polos with our club name embroidered in green. My friend and Saffron's co-raiser, Kelly, had suggested yellow. "Yellow is a happy color and these dogs make people happy," she said to justify her suggestion. "And besides, most of our dogs are yellow Labs. It will hide the hair."

Made perfect sense to me, so yellow it was. Even Jon donned a yellow shirt. Saffron was gone by now. She had graduated the previous fall and was now a working guide. Tartan, too. Each parade, we have a new set of dogs. This year, I held the leash on Delancey, my new pup and the only black Lab in our group. Her black hair really stood out on that yellow shirt. Oh well.

At 11 A.M. sharp, Sheriff Main signaled the parade to begin. The Sweet Sensations' theme song started up again, and the little girls with frozen-on smiles shimmied down the road. Jon kick-started the

Cushman, and we were off.

At the corner, I recognized Mr. Hastings, a Lions Club member. A few weeks earlier I had spoken at his noon club meeting about our program. They gave us a nice donation. I broke ranks to run over to shake his hand and say hello.

The crowd (or at least the males who were of the right age to appreciate a '50s scooter) gave Jon "thumbs up" as he passed. He sat up a little straighter and waved.

In front of the judges' stand we executed an obedience routine of sits and turns, as Jon idled on his scooter. A couple of men from the sidelines sauntered up to more closely admire Jon's handiwork. He proudly showed it off.

As we finished our routine with a synchronized "sit," I glanced over at Jon. He was looking at me. Our eyes met and we smiled.

I don't know if it was the yellow polo shirts or the synchronized sit or Jon's scooter, but we won the Director's Choice Award.

That evening in the garage, Jon carefully draped the scooter with a dust cover. I retreated upstairs to return some phone calls. By the time I came back downstairs, it was late. Riley snored on his bed in the corner of the kitchen. The television lit the darkened living room with flickering bluish light. I heard Jon before I saw him.

"You were such a good girl today," he said as he stroked

Delancey's ears. He was sitting on the living-room floor. Delancey was stretched out next to him, half-asleep, with her head on his thigh.

I watched silently. It had been a good day. Both of us had engaged in our separate hobbies, but we had found a way to combine and enjoy them together. I was proud of his finely restored Cushman; he was pleased with how well my dogs performed.

Our differences are what make us special to each other. Jon gives me room to pursue my interests; I do the same for him. And we appreciate and respect the other's achievements. By doing so, we keep our love alive. ❖

※

November 14

Dear Kilroy,

We just returned from our walk. There was a new dog on our route. She has light, light blue eyes. I was so interested in her that I walked into a mailbox. I wasn't hurt—just embarrassed. Wow, is she cute. Sigh.

Love,

Riley

※

November 16

Dear Riley,

    Forget her. There's nothing you can do about it anyway.

Love,

Kilroy

Jesse fills his lap.

We are alone, absolutely alone on this planet;
and amid all the forms of life that surround us,
not one, excepting the dog has made an alliance with us.
—MAURICE MAETERLINCK

❋

A HOME FOR JESSE

When my mother died, we encouraged our father to get a pet. His answer was succinct and always the same: "No way."

In our family while I was growing up, Dad barely tolerated the pets that inhabited our house. My two turtles. My sister's poodle. My brother's mice. My sister's parakeet. And the family cats. We always had a cat, at least one. There was Buttons, the calico; Mister, the tabby (previously known as "Missy," until a better understanding of his anatomy prompted a name change); and Sam and Ping Pong, the black cats. Dad's relationship with our cats never varied. He'd wave his arms and say "pssssssssst" each time he saw them. They'd scurry for cover. Before long, the cats learned it was best to stay out of his way.

Dad was seventy-five when Mom died. They had known each other since he was nine and she was eight. Dad grew up in a family of three boys; our family totaled six, plus cousins, aunts, uncles, and Grandma—all who lived close enough to visit often. Until Mom went to a care facility, Dad had never lived alone.

There is a quietness in an empty house that echoes even louder when the occupant remembers how it used to be. There are sounds, but they are mostly mechanical—not the sounds of the living. The ticking of a clock replaces laughter. The whir of the washing machine substitutes for the noisy chatter of morning. The hum of the refrigerator takes the place of quiet bedtime murmurs. These sounds exist in every home, but when they are the only sounds, they are the sounds of loneliness.

When I visited Dad, he'd comment, "I'm glad you're here. It's so nice to have someone to talk to." Of course, that made me feel bad and guilty. My sisters, brother, and I included him in many activities, but I know he missed simple, day-to-day interactions. Someone to talk to. Someone to say good night to.

On Father's Day, we shared brunch at my favorite riverside lodge. "Dad, you know if you find someone new, we'd all be very happy for you," I said. "Mom wouldn't want you to be alone."

He nodded but changed the subject. I didn't mention it again.

A few years later, we learned that a (widowed) friend from Dad's college days was stopping by his house each time she passed through his city on the way to visit her children. Alice and I gossiped over it. "Do you think it's more than friendship?" we'd wonder aloud to each other.

Then, the visits stopped. Months later, Dad shared a letter from her. "Read this," he said. The letter was a few months old—dated about the time her visits to him ceased. The letter was uplifting, but painful, and was addressed to her many friends. She wrote that she had been diagnosed with an aggressive, terminal illness. It was her good-bye to them all.

"She died about a month after I got this letter," Dad said. He carefully folded it up again, following the creases already made. He gently returned it to its envelope. "When she visited me, I asked her if she ever thought about getting married again," he said quietly, his eyes cast down. "Now, it doesn't matter what her answer was."

After that, he seemed to give up on finding another soul mate. "She was my last chance," he said simply, and that was that.

He retreated further into himself. His hobby has always been trains—model trains, riding trains, building trains. That's all he did. That's all he talked about. He started giving away his things. He asked me to go through his papers with him, to "get them in order."

His temper got shorter, his smiles fewer. His laughter all but disappeared. At times, our patience with him stretched thin, but this was a man who always had cared for us and did his very best as our father. We never once doubted his love. He deserved our loyalty, no matter what. His life had been devoted to us and helping others. He had taught high school math, history, and industrial arts. He had once taught at a school for the deaf and, in the summers, at a youth prison.

In July, on my mother's birthday (she would have been eighty-one), Dad and I talked on the phone. Although neither of us acknowledged the date, he knew why I had called. I always call on the special days. I talked, and he grumbled about nothing in particular.

A few days later, I volunteered at our animal shelter. My friend Cheryl and I walked through the kennels with a heavy heart, knowing that many of the animals would not be adopted. We vowed to place at least two that day.

I picked a four-month-old black Labrador (he looked a lot like Riley); Cheryl picked a small, white dog I thought was a Pomeranian.

"No, no, Nora, don't you know your breeds?" she chided me. "It's a miniature American Eskimo." The tag on his kennel read "Jesse."

We played with the dogs out in the exercise yard. The black Lab promptly started retrieving sticks. Jesse danced around on his back legs, waving his front paws in the air. We laughed at their antics and returned with them to the office to work the phones, calling everyone we knew. Cheryl concentrated on care facilities.

"This little guy will make some older person very happy," she said as she pulled him up into her lap. Jesse settled in, quite content to be a lap dog.

A voice in my head said: *Dad*.

I ignored it.

"I'm surprised no one has taken you home, yet," Cheryl said, as she stroked Jesse's head. The smaller breeds usually find homes fairly easily. They rarely last long at the shelter. But Jesse had been there for more than a week already.

Cheryl hung up from her last call. "Nope, no luck. Sorry, Jesse."

I made calls for the Lab and got quite a bit of interest. Several promised to stop by to meet him. I watched Cheryl play with Jesse. His face seemed frozen in a perpetual smile. His dark eyes sparkled.

This time the voice came from my heart: *Dad*.

But Dad doesn't want a pet, I argued with myself. *But . . . maybe for just two weeks*, I argued back. I picked up the phone and called Dad.

" . . . and he's been here eight days," I concluded. "Can you keep him for two weeks while we try to find him a home?"

He did not hesitate. "Bring him up," he said. His reply surprised me, but it really shouldn't have. Jesse needed someone, and Dad always responded to someone in need.

I made arrangements quickly. Lin, my friend who had recently adopted Grace, said she'd accompany me on the two-hour drive to Dad's house. I appreciated the offer.

Dad greeted us in his front yard. It was not love at first sight. I handed him Jesse's leash, and Dad walked tentatively, holding the leash out awkwardly. I was glad to see that Jesse did not pull or get himself tangled in Dad's legs.

Inside the house, Dad immediately invited Lin to see his trains in the garage. Jesse was forgotten, but he followed them into the garage anyway.

I wrote out feeding, relieving, and exercise instructions. We couldn't stay long. As we left, Dad said, "Now, you'll be back in two weeks, right? I can't keep him any longer." I assured him I'd be back.

Lin was confident Dad would keep Jesse. I wasn't. "Dad has never been a pet person," I told her.

I made good on my promise and continued to look for a home for Jesse. I called friends and notified my network of guide-dog volunteers. Everyone assured me that it would be easy. But no one came forward with a home.

Several days passed, and Dad still insisted I come for Jesse. But slowly, the canine magic began to work. Dad started to wonder what would happen to Jesse if no home were found.

"He'll get a few more days at the shelter," I explained. "I hope someone will adopt him. If not . . . ," I paused, not liking what I knew

I had to say. "He'll be euthanized," I said finally. It was that simple. Too many dogs.

The next night, Dad called again. This time he talked enthusiastically about how Jesse followed him around the house and how he'd sit in his lap. He laughed when he described how Jesse could dance on his hind legs.

Finally, ten days after I dropped Jesse off, Dad called and said, "Your sister thinks I should keep Jesse."

"What do *you* think?" I replied.

I know that with pet adoptions the new owner must truly want the pet for it to be a successful match. Alice had been dropping by his house every evening. She, too, was taken by Jesse's sweetness.

"Well, he's no trouble at all," Dad said. Then he added, "I'd like to keep him." My heart sang. There was a lightness in Dad's voice that I had not heard in a long time.

Dad's commitment was immediate and strong. With Alice's help, he arranged a complete vet exam, including neutering, a dog grooming, and the purchase of more supplies.

More than two weeks had passed since I first dropped off Jesse. Alice and Dad—and Jesse—met me at a restaurant as I drove through their town on my way home from Portland. Dad proudly showed off Jesse's new summer hair cut. Jesse looked like an adorable stuffed animal. He wore a bright-red harness.

"The collar tends to slip over his little head," Dad explained. "This works better. I don't want to lose him."

I snapped a picture of them. In the photo, Dad's arms encircle Jesse protectively, and his right hand cradles Jesse's front paw.

He asked me how long a dog like Jesse could live. Jesse was about four, so I told Dad he had probably ten years, maybe more. "I hope he outlives me," he said softly.

Dad's house is not as quiet anymore. Occasionally, Jesse barks when he sees a stranger outside. The jingle of his tags and the click of his toenails on the wood floors drown out the ticking of the clock.

Each morning, Jesse wakes Dad by placing his front paws on the edge of Dad's bed. His smile lights the day. He follows Dad around the house and dances when Dad brings out his leash for a walk.

When he works on his model trains, Jesse lies quietly and listens intently as Dad explains what he is doing. In the evenings, they watch television. Jesse fills Dad's lap, or sometimes they lie on the floor, curled up together. At night, they retire to the bedroom—Dad to his queen-sized bed, Jesse to his little dog bed next to Dad's.

As the house settles into darkness and before sleep takes over, Dad quietly murmurs, "Good night, Jesse." And the room fills with the soft sounds of their breathing. ❖

※

November 18

Dear Kilroy,

Mom puppy-sat one of your guide-dog cousins all last week. She was a cute thing . . . a black Lab / golden retriever cross. Like me, only lots smaller. She weighs forty pounds. She's nice. She wanted to sleep next to me all the time. I let her put her elbow on my bed. Next thing I knew she had edged me off my bed and was snorin' with her head on my back.

I'm looking forward to your visit when your mom goes on vacation. You can sleep near me, but bring your own bed.

Love,

Riley

※

November 21

Dear Mom,

Sure hope you're having fun in Hawaii with Shane and Tessa. I'm having a great time here with cousin Riley, Uncle Jon, and Auntie Nora. We go for walks every day. I also take long naps in the kitchen with Riley.

Yesterday, Auntie Nora came in and disappeared up the stairs. I'd never been upstairs before, so I decided to check it out. I found her in a big shower. I stuck my head in. The water felt nice and warm. Her head was all sudsy, and her eyes were closed. I think I surprised her because when she opened her eyes, she screamed.

So I went on back to the kitchen. No harm done. Just some wet dog prints down the stairs.

I miss you.

Love,

Kilroy

I stuck
my head in.

*Mecca, a yellow Lab with
gray around the muzzle.*

I guide you in the way of wisdom
and lead you along straight paths.
—PROVERBS 4:11

❧

VICKI AND MECCA

Vicki does not know I am watching her. She and Mecca, her guide dog, descend from the bus. On the sidewalk, Mecca gives a good shake. A small cloud of yellow hair explodes around her. She wags her tail happily. Vicki lifts Mecca's harness handle and gives her the "forward" command. They walk together in a harmony of motion. Quickly. Confidently.

The first time I saw a guide-dog team work, I was amazed at how fast they walked. Guide-dog handlers often express the same reaction the first time they work with a dog; they compare it to flying. With a white cane, the progress is slower and more tentative.

And no matter how many times I see a guide-dog team, I always feel a bit of awe. Human and dog dance a subtle ballet of footwork, hand motions, and voice commands. As I watch, Mecca leads Vicki around a streetlight pole, leaving room for Vicki to clear. I doubt Vicki is even aware what Mecca has done.

The last time Vicki and I had lunch, Saffron, my guide pup in training, joined us. Today, for this lunch date, black Lab Delancey in her green coat accompanies me. I call out to my friend, saying my name to let her know I am there. We greet with a hug and Mecca, who always knows a dog person, jiggles with excitement. But when we turn to walk toward my car, she's all business again.

Mecca, a yellow Lab with gray around the muzzle, and Vicki walk in graceful synchronization. More than seven years ago, guide-dog trainers specifically selected Mecca for Vicki based on her size, temperament, pace, and Vicki's lifestyle. The two trained together for weeks under the watchful eye of an instructor. Vicki received the training, Mecca, and a lifetime of vet care for no charge.

Guide Dogs for the Blind receives no government funding. The organization, including its professional staff, is financed by generous donors and supported by about two thousand volunteers.

Vicki is a slender, youthful woman of fifty-some years. Her shoulder-length brown hair sets off a helping of freckles across her face. Guide dogs have been a part of her life for more than twenty-five years, since her doctor declared her legally blind at the age of twenty-three.

"That's when I lost my peripheral vision. Over the years, the rest of my vision has gone," she once told me. "Getting a guide dog gave me confidence, freedom, and dignity."

She and her husband, a retired fire chief, raised twins—a boy and a girl. Vicki trained with her first guide dog shortly after the twins were born. Even though Vicki could see somewhat in front of her, she still qualified for a guide dog. With no side vision, she could not safely cross a street or even navigate a parking lot by foot. It's a common misconception that only the completely blind use guide dogs.

Her husband's recent retirement means the two of them, now empty-nesters, have more time to sail their boat through the Pacific waters off Oregon and Washington. Mecca sails with them.

It was near their boat many years ago that Vicki first cemented the trust with Mecca that is so important to their teamwork.

"We were in a port I know very well. It has a lovely boardwalk," Vicki explains. "I know the route by heart and often took evening strolls with only Mecca. We came to a junction where I always turn right to loop back to our starting point. Mecca stopped. I gave her the 'right' command, but she refused to go forward. I gave the command louder with more insistence.

"But she still wouldn't move. I knew we needed to turn right, and I was getting mad. I waved my arm in exasperation. Something snagged my hand. It was construction flagging," Vicki says sheepishly.

Gingerly, she put her toe forward and felt a drop off. Later, her husband told her the area was torn up for new sewer pipes. Mecca had refused to let Vicki walk off into a five-foot-deep trench, demonstrating one of the most important components of her training: intelligent disobedience. It's not too difficult to teach a dog to unquestioningly follow a handler's commands; it's something else to teach a dog to make decisions and know when to disobey. Not all dogs are capable of learning this skill.

Mecca walks a little slower these days. But whenever Vicki pulls out her harness, Mecca acts like the puppy she once was. Vicki knows that in the not-too-distant future, Mecca will retire as a guide. She dreads it, for Mecca is not just a guide, but a well-loved companion and best friend. When the time comes, Mecca will go live with Vicki's mother as a cherished pet. And Vicki will return to the Guide Dogs for the Blind campus. She will spend several weeks training with her new guide dog. It will be her sixth.

That afternoon when I return to my office, I brush Mecca's yellow hairs from my pants and settle into my chair. Delancey snoozes on Saffron's old blue rug next to my desk. She curls up tightly, her nose tucked into her tail, her back pressed against my filing cabinet. Her sides expand and contract in the gentle rhythm of her breathing. This pup represents the best of her breed. Saffron is her aunt; Kilroy, Tartan, and Nash are distant cousins. I wonder if she will grow up to be Vicki's next guide dog. ❖

※

November 25

Dear Nora,

Today is Thanksgiving, an appropriate day to write you. "Thank you" does not seem like a strong enough expression for what I want to share, but know that these two simple words hold much gratitude.

This week as Saffron was guiding me to the bus stop, we started to cross a wide driveway. Very suddenly, she backed up—hard, pushing me backward. Then a car zoomed out, just inches from us. I had no idea that the car was coming, but Saffron did. She saved my life.

Besides being my guardian angel, Saffron has taken on a second job. The folks at the senior day-care center (where I volunteer) love her. Many there suffer from dementia. Once we get to the center, I take off her harness, and she visits the seniors.

One gentleman who is confined to a wheelchair is quite confused and thinks Saffron is his old dog "Molly." Saffron sits next to him and puts her head on his armrest so he can pet her. Saffron is the only one who can make him smile.

For our vacation, Saffron and I visited Disneyland. She guided me through the crowds, and we even went on some rides together. Saffron's favorite was "It's a Small World." We slowly floated through the ride in a large boat, while small dancing figures sang. Saffron loved the singing. Others in the boat said she sat calmly, cocked her head, and listened.

I know you gave your heart to Saffron. For a year, you nurtured her and helped mold her. You loved her. Then, you gave her up. Saffron is my gift from heaven, my friend, my companion. She gives me freedom and courage.

Thank you.

Your friend,
Colleen

☼

November 28

Dear Kilroy,

Mom got a letter from Saffron's blind partner today. She sat on my bed next to me and read it out loud. When she was done reading, she was quiet for a little bit and wiped her eyes.

"I'm so proud of Saffron," she said finally. "She's really good at being a guide." Then she started rubbing the little bump on top of my head. "And I'm so glad that you are our dog, Riley. Our very own special Riley."

I let out a big sigh, so she knew I felt the same way.

You know, Kilroy, you and I will never get to go to Disneyland the way Saffron did, but that's okay. Our jobs are right where we are.

Love,

Riley

He shook happily.

The most affectionate creature
in the world is a wet dog.
—AMBROSE BIERCE

❧

SUMMER

Jon's favorite season in Oregon is fall. The maple and sycamore trees around our house explode into fiery reds, yellows, and oranges set against a solid-green background of pine trees. The fishing is good, and the hint of wood smoke permeates the morning air. The warm days dissolve into crisp, cool nights. He adds an extra blanket to the bed, so we can still keep the window open to hear the river at night.

I prefer spring. Maybe it's because by April I'm tired of the short days and overcast skies. The pink plum-tree blossoms and yellow daffodils reassure me that winter is done and new life cycles begin again. And the green. I never knew so many shades of green existed before I moved to Oregon. The lime green of new growth on the tips of the pines. The darker green of budding oak leaves dressing the naked branches of winter. The yellow-green of freshly sprouted grass cloaking the surrounding hills.

Sometimes, Jon and I argue good naturedly over which season is the best. When our voices rise in mock anger, Riley comes to us. He does not like us to argue. His eyebrows rise, first one then the other, as he looks back and forth between us, and we can't help but giggle. The "argument" is over.

Riley, ever the diplomat, would never take sides in the which-season-is-best debate. No, I think he'd probably weigh in with his own vote . . . for summer.

He literally kicks up his heels for summer. He flips backside down and rubs and twists his spine on the cool lawn, pointing all fours skyward as he gyrates in joy.

Summer means the river warms to swimming and rafting temperatures. He wades in like a hippopotamus, his back just breaking the surface, his tail floating out behind. He takes bites of water, slurping it in. I throw several sticks which he pursues with determination. He'll bring back one, then two, and maybe a third, all at the same time. A friend called Riley a show-off as he returned to me with two sticks and a Frisbee in his mouth. But I know better. Riley is simply doing what he loves: retrieving.

I once took Max, my first dog, out in our inflatable river raft. I think the undulating motion made him seasick. He lasted only a few moments before he jumped overboard. I assumed that Riley would do the same.

One summer day, when Riley was about a year old, I pushed off in the raft. Riley ran back and forth along the water's edge, not taking his eyes off me. As I paddled away, he could stand it no longer. He leaped into the water. A few powerful strokes brought him to the raft, and he began clawing at it, trying to get in. Worried that his nails would puncture the side, I grasped him beneath his front legs and heaved as hard as I could. We both tumbled back onto the floor of the raft. He recovered his balance and shook happily, drenching me in water and wet, black hair that stuck to my bare legs. Then, he settled comfortably at the front, his head hanging over the raft's side, which served as a bolster for his massive head. He was content and not going anywhere except with me.

Each summer, Riley and I raft together, both of us tightly cinched into our matching, yellow life jackets. We lazily drift through the ranch lands dried golden by the summer sun. Clusters of pine and fir trees rise and pierce the blinding blue of the sky. At times, the paddling gets tiresome, and I slightly resent that Riley lies sleepily in the boat like a ninety-pound anchor. He provides no power to help us through the dead-calm areas.

But Riley has other, more important jobs. He serves as the perfect nature guide. His keen vision and sense of smell home in on the wildlife around us. When his body tenses, I merely follow his line of sight. There, at the shore, a mother duck weaves her way though the water grass, a line of ducklings at her rear. When his gaze turns up, I, too, look to heaven. An osprey glides silently searching the river for dinner. Then we both glance to the other shore as a flock of Canada geese honk back and forth.

The current picks up as we approach an outcropping of rocks that cut across the river. The rushing water here emits a dull roar, getting louder and louder as we get nearer. The elevation dips, and the water seeks channels to power around and over the rocks. I paddle hard to keep control, to keep the raft headed straight through the largest chute of water. My heartbeat quickens, but Riley still lies calmly at the front.

A surge pushes the raft slightly sideways. I struggle unsuccessfully to keep the nose pointed directly into the chute. The water lifts up the side, we're tipping, we're going over. I'm underwater kicking. My life vest does its job and pops me to the surface. My floatable flip-flop sandals tumble away in the waves, out of reach. Then Riley is there. He strokes like an Olympic swimmer. He pursues the sandals. He grabs one, then the other in his mouth, then makes for shore. I clasp the rope of the raft and start kicking hard. My awkward paddling and splashing and dragging eventually get me and the raft to shore, where Riley waits, dripping, happily panting, and proudly standing over the sandals.

Riley is thirteen now, and he doesn't swim as gracefully anymore. His joints have stiffened with arthritis. On hot summer days, I try to get our walk in early. I slow my pace to match his. We walk to a spot at the river where he can wade in easily.

Summer showers occasionally cool off our parched hills. And when they do, they leave behind a sky-embracing rainbow. In the guide-dog community, when a dog dies we say he has crossed over the rainbow bridge. There he will wait for his human to join him. When I imagine that bridge, I picture it spanning our river. It's easy to envision—a rainbow bridge stretching from one golden hillside across the river to another.

When the time comes for Riley to cross that bridge, I'm sure there will be only one season on the other side—summer. ❖

Where I belong.

✳

April 9

Dear Riley,

Thank you for the chew bone. Mom made me a birthday cake, but she and her friend ate most of it. Guess she didn't want a repeat of The Blackberry Incident. I like Mom's friend; he's nice and very good to her. It's hard to believe that I'm three years old now. I can barely remember that I ever wore the green jacket and that I was training to be a guide dog.

But you know what? I don't think I was *supposed* to be a guide dog. I think I was always supposed to find Mom and be hers forever. She needed me so much that day I came into her life. I remember she was waiting for me in a big room with supper dishes. And it was filled with dog food. It smelled like heaven. She called to me like she had known me for all time. Since this room was heaven, I figured she must be an angel. She smelled even better than dog food, so I gave her a big kiss.

I've learned a lot since then:

- Don't drag flower pots around the patio.
- Phone boxes are not food.
- Eat blackberries in moderation.

I love Mom even more than I did that first day, if that's possible. When she comes home from work, I do the Happy Dance to let her know how much I missed her. When she goes to bed, I kiss her good night. When she wakes up, I make sure my face is the first thing she sees. It's hard to imagine a time before we were together. I know I'm where I belong.

Love,

Kilroy

*They help us
make friends.*

A dog is the only thing on earth who
loves you more than you love yourself.
—JOSH BILLINGS

❧

EPILOGUE

$\mathcal{O}$*ur puppy-raising club hit a high of ten puppies* this month. Yellow Lab Nash still hangs out at the printing company. The business has tripled in size, which means more people come and go. More people to rub his tummy. More people to scratch his ears. Sherry's two daughters have grown and left home, so it's just Nash and her in the evenings. He keeps her feet warm while she crochets.

Lacey continues to fill Renee's house with strawberry-golden retriever hair. "Nora, you did not tell me about all the shedding," Renee jokingly commented to me recently. A small price for the love Lacey gives to Renee's family. My success with matching Lacey with Renee and Jesse with Dad led me to help with other pet adoptions. I've placed many since then. When folks ask me about adopting a guide-dog career-change pup, I encourage them to fill out the application. But I also send them to the animal shelter. There are so many wonderful dogs (and cats) put down every year for lack of a home.

At the Saving Grace Pet Adoption Center, the sheer volume of unwanted animals sometimes overwhelms our little facility, the staff, and our volunteers. A few weeks ago, Sheriff Main confiscated ninety cats and fifty dogs from one individual and brought them to our shelter for care; some needed emergency vet services. We continue to plan our new building, but just day-to-day operations can challenge even those with the best intentions. Until the public understands the need to spay and neuter pets and that adopting a pet is a lifetime commitment, shelters will struggle. It's a huge job, and our experience only gives me greater empathy for those who work and volunteer for the humane treatment of animals.

Rob in Seattle expects he and Tartan will be a "very mobile team" for many years. They are well into building the bond that is so important to their partnership. "Tartan has learned my frequent routes and intuitively locates some of my favorite haunts," he wrote to Lesley in his Christmas letter (apparently, Rob loves his Starbucks, and Tartan knows it). In honor of the holiday season, Rob bought him a tartan scarf, which Tartan wears grudgingly. Lesley recently welcomed her third guide pup into her home.

My wedding photo with Mom sits on my dresser, where I see it each morning. I especially feel her presence when we take our guide pups to nursing homes. As I watch the residents interact happily with the dogs, I know, somewhere, Mom is well again and smiling.

I took Colleen and Saffron to lunch a couple of weeks ago. Sometimes I think about the old saying regarding marrying off a daughter: You don't lose a daughter; you gain a son. I feel that way about Colleen and Saffron. I didn't lose my dog; I gained a friend. We see each other at guide-dog functions or occasionally when I am in the Portland area. Colleen is taking a class in independent living. I did not know it when I first met her, but she has never lived on her own. So many things that sighted people take for granted are challenges for the blind. She's had more than her share to overcome, and she's taking them one at a time. Living on her own has been a longtime dream. Getting Saffron was the first step to realizing it. I am constantly inspired by Colleen's upbeat attitude.

Black Lab Delancey leaves us next month to begin her formal training to become a guide. Her black hairs now mingle with Saffron's platinum hairs in the blue rug next to my desk. No matter how many times I vacuum it, a few dog hairs remain. I kind of like it that way.

Dad's relationship with Jesse has blossomed into full-blown love. When he visits my brother, Frank, in Boston, he hurries home after a week. "I don't want Jesse to think I've left him too long," he told me. Six months after getting Jesse, Dad decided to move into a senior community. I believe it's because Jesse helped Dad reengage life. I told Dad I'd help him pick out a place. He had only one condition: "They must accept dogs." Within six weeks, Alice, Frank, Kathie, and I helped him sort his belongings, sell his house, and move into a comfortable two-bedroom apartment in a retirement village that welcomes pets. The women-to-men ratio there is four-to-one. Who knows what will happen.

My friend Vicki retired her guide dog Mecca not long ago. Mecca now lives the life of a pampered pet. Her vet bills are taken care of for life, thanks to her guide-dog "pension." Guide Dogs for the Blind never forgets the service these dogs provide and makes sure they are cared for as long as they live. Vicki has a new guide, a petite golden retriever named Parsley. This summer, Vicki and her husband discovered the fun of riding a tandem bicycle. They pull Parsley behind them in a bike trailer.

Riley sleeps a lot these days. He no longer can manage our fourteen-mile hikes, but he's capable of a three-mile walk along the river. I have to hold him back a bit—the spirit is willing, while the body is not.

Alice is as happy as I've ever seen her. She and her fiance are building a new home on the outskirts of her town, complete with a dog-friendly play yard. They will marry this summer. Kilroy can't wait. He's going to be the ring bearer.

Researchers tell us that pets improve our human immune-system functions—a fancy way to say they make us feel good. But I don't need researchers to know that. I only need to look at Dad while he holds Jesse in his lap. His large, calloused hands gently stroke the top of Jesse's little head. Jesse's eyes droop sleepily, and Dad settles deeper into his overstuffed sofa with a sigh.

I watch Vicki play tug with her guide dog Parsley, who play-growls as she throws herself into the game. Vicki laughs gleefully then pulls Parsley to her for a hug. Vicki can't see Parsley with her eyes; she sees Parsley with her heart.

After a stressful day, I feel my own blood pressure drop as I sit on the floor with Riley with his head in my lap.

Kilroy may have "failed" at becoming a guide dog for the blind. Instead, he became the guide for Alice on her journey from sorrow to new happiness. When she felt unloved, unsafe, and unhappy, he gave her affection, security, and laughter. Kilroy taught us that success takes many forms.

Yes, dogs make us feel good. They help us make friends, transcend tragedies, grieve the loss of loved ones, and just plain enjoy life. They improve our physical health and our mental health. They walk beside us as our buddies, partners, and teachers. They are our guides through life. ❖

Guide dog puppies.

Guide dogs do more than just keep
their blind handlers from walking aimlessly
across busy intersections. At times, our dogs also
keep us from walking aimlessly through life.

— KEVIN FRANKEBERGER

❖

REFERENCES

Since I work with guide-dog puppies in public, people frequently ask me questions about the organization, dogs, and even blindness. I have learned that training the pups is only one part of my volunteer effort; another very important part is public education.

Guide Dogs for the Blind was founded in 1942 to serve blind World War II veterans. It operates two training facilities, one in San Rafael, California, and one in Boring, Oregon. The organization provides guide dogs and training in their use to visually impaired people in the United States and Canada. The person must be legally blind and over sixteen years old (there is no upper limit). The dogs and the training are provided at no charge. The organization receives no government funding, but instead relies on the generosity of donors and the support of volunteers.

Guide Dogs for the Blind adheres to the Humane Training Standards developed and promoted by the United States Council of Dog Guide Schools.

Applicants are screened via home interviews and reference checks, and when in class, the students receive in-depth training in the appropriate care and treatment of their dogs.

To learn more about volunteering, adopting a career-change dog, receiving a guide dog, or attending a graduation ceremony (they are open to the public), contact Guide Dogs for the Blind or visit its web site.

Guide Dogs for the Blind
(800) 295-4050, www.guidedogs.com, P.O. Box 151200, San Rafael, CA 94915

The Saving Grace Pet Adoption Center, a nonprofit organization, was founded to champion, promote, and protect the human-animal bond through responsible pet ownership. Staff and volunteers work diligently to educate the public about proper animal care and that euthanasia is not the answer to pet overpopulation.

Saving Grace Pet Adoption Center, P.O. Box 803, Winchester, OR 97495

The following organizations and companies provide good, general information for anyone interested in learning more about training, volunteering, or caring for our canine friends. For direct links to some of these sites, check out **www.dearkilroy.com**.

Assistance Dogs International
www.adionline.org, 980 Everett St., Lakewood, CO 80215

When people ask me about service dogs for disabilities other than blindness, I refer them to Assistance Dogs International, a coalition of not-for-profit organizations that train and place assistance dogs. The member list, posted on the web site, provides contact information for more than fifty organizations. It also publishes a handy booklet which summarizes the legal rights of service dogs.

American Kennel Club
(919) 233-9767, www.akc.org, 5580 Centerview Dr., Raleigh, NC 27606

If your dog is registered with the American Kennel Club, you can buy his or her family tree at the AKC web site; click on "Shop AKC." That's how I discovered Kilroy and Saffron were first cousins. General information on all registered breeds also is included, which can be very helpful when selecting a dog for a pet.

American Society for the Prevention of Cruelty to Animals
(212) 876-7700, www.aspca.org, 424 E. 92nd St., New York, NY 10128

Some flea-control products that are safely used on dogs can be deadly to cats, warns the ASPCA Animal Poison Control Center, which posts warnings and informational articles on its site.

The Humane Society of the United States
(202) 452-1100, www.hsus.org, www.animalsheltering.org
2100 L St. NW, Washington, DC 20037

If you are involved with an animal shelter, humane society, or animal-control agency, visit Animal Sheltering Online, a web site from The Humane Society of the United States. The site offers everything from sample forms to back issues of its magazine. When we had a parvovirus outbreak at our shelter, the information provided by this resource was invaluable.

Drs. Foster & Smith
(800) 381-7179, www.drsfostersmith.com, P.O. Box 100, Rhinelander, WI 54501

Not only does this company provide a wide selection of pet supplies, it's a cornucopia of pet information. I've always appreciated the concise, well-written articles about pet-health issues in the catalog and on the web site. You'll find the basics ("How much should you feed your pet?") as well as the not so basic ("How to prevent seizures in gerbils").

PETCO
(800) 571-2952, www.petco.com, 9125 Rehco Rd., San Diego, CA 92121

The philanthropic arm of PETCO, the PETCO Foundation, promotes charitable, educational, and other philanthropic activities for the betterment of companion animals. The foundation focuses on the "Four Rs": Reduce, Rescue, Rehabilitate, Rejoice. Applications for support are available online.

PETsMART
(888) 839-9638, www.petsmart.com, P.O. Box 910, Brockport, NY 14420

Through PETsMART Charities, this pet-supplies company works to save pets' lives and end the use of euthanasia as a means of pet population control. In-store space is made available for shelters to showcase homeless animals.

The Iams Company
(800) 675-3849, www.iams.com, 7250 Poe Ave., Dayton, OH 45414

The Iams web site offers interactive responses. Type in your question, and information is supplied tailored to your specific situation. The questionnaire to help a family select the right dog breed for a pet is especially helpful.

Nestlé Purina Pet Care
(314) 982-1000, www.purina.com, Checkerboard Square, St. Louis, MO 63164

It's not only about pet food. Purina offers advice on behavior and training issues, too. Is your neighbor's dog a "bark machine"? Learn ways to modify the dog's (and the neighbor's) behavior on the Purina web site.

Pfizer Animal Health Product Support
(800) 366-5288, www.pfizer.com, 235 East 42nd Street, New York, NY 10017

As Riley has aged, his care needs have changed. Pfizer dedicates a portion of its web site to the senior dog. I've implemented several of the suggestions: raising Riley's food dish to lessen the strain on his neck and back, adding a dog-safe heating pad under his bed, keeping him at his optimal weight, and giving him a medication to ease his arthritis. The advances in veterinary medicine are remarkable, and I'm thankful as they help bring longer life to our dear friends.

Science Diet
(800) 445-5777, www.sciencediet.com
Hill's Pet Nutrition, P.O. Box 148, Topeka, KS 66601

Interesting fact: This company was founded more than fifty years ago when Dr. Mark L. Morris Sr., a veterinarian, responded to a young blind man's request for help in saving his guide dog, who was suffering from kidney disease. The result of Dr. Morris's efforts was the nutritional formulation that would become the first Hill's Prescription Diet product. Since then, the company has formulated a line of products to address specific dietary needs.

Guide pup
Ashton.

A dog desires affection more than its dinner.
Well . . . almost.

—CHARLOTTE GRAY

❦

ACKNOWLEDGMENTS

As I write this, Riley is sticking his nose under my hands and trying to throw them off my computer keyboard. It is 5 P.M. He is hungry and expects to be fed.

To Riley and Kilroy I owe my first thanks. Even though they often distracted me to come and play, they also nurtured and inspired me to write. I gratefully acknowledge ALICE VITZ TUCKER, big sister and friend. She not only helped give Kilroy a voice, she encouraged me to express my own through this book.

I'd like to thank the people who allowed me to tell their stories. In a few cases, I changed names and details for privacy reasons.

Thank you to all service-dog raisers and my guide-dog raising club, current and past members. They unselfishly give of themselves so that others will benefit. I am grateful for ANIMAL SHELTERS everywhere and the people who work to ensure the humane treatment of dogs and other animals.

PAT COOK, puppy-raising adviser and trainer extraordinaire for Guide Dogs for the Blind, taught me that before you can train a dog, you must first speak his language. She is the most fluent human speaker of "Dog" I have ever met. Thank you to all of the other employees of Guide Dogs for the Blind who come to work each day not because it is their job, but because it is their passion.

I appreciate the support of LYNN HOBBS, fellow puppy-raising leader, especially during the early days of our club. And thank you to another leader, TERRI JO MORGAN, and the MILLER FAMILY, who gave Kilroy such a great start in life.

Years ago, I took every writing class offered by BRUCE MCALLISTER; I am very fortunate to have reconnected with Bruce—my teacher, editor, coach, and friend. I am also grateful to the friends who reviewed early drafts of this book and gave me encouragement. You know who you are.

My love and thanks to JON HARRISON, who patiently accepts the parade of dogs I bring through our home.

Finally, I give my love to EVERY GUIDE PUP and especially the ones who have passed through our club: Jasper, Nash, Marcy, Maggie, Evita, Shiloh, Gary, Bram, Lena, Jargon, Fax, Flick, Saffron, Silky, Kovax, Gisela, Auburn, Tartan, Nelson, Nickie, Dembe, Dorinda, Rex, Simona, Cinder, Bertha, Glendale, Michelle, Delancey, Mannix, Lundy, Ulysses, Ashton, Alya, Niner, Tempo, Crissy, Shawnee, Jacoba, Herman, Pitney, Tanya, Valentino, Louwilla, Waldie, and Rigley. They taught us more than we could ever teach them.

And now, I really must go feed Riley. ❖

About the author:

*N*ORA *VITZ HARRISON* is a longtime volunteer for Guide Dogs for the Blind and active in animal-welfare organizations. She has been a writer for corporate America since 1979. Her human-interest essays have been published in *The Oregonian* newspaper and other publications. *Dear Kilroy* is her first book. She lives in Oregon with her husband, Jon, and her dog, Riley. When she is not writing, she likes to hike, which is Riley's favorite hobby, too.

Kilroy's correspondence contributed in part by Alice Vitz Tucker.

*A*LICE *VITZ TUCKER* works at Oregon State University. She lives in Corvallis, Oregon, with her husband, Ron; two children; and Kilroy, a yellow Labrador retriever. She enjoys theater and playing the piano, accompanied by Kilroy on vocals.